Nonverbal Learning Disabilities at Home

Companion volume

Nonverbal Learning Disabilities at School
Educating Students with NLD, Asperger Syndrome and Related Conditions
Pamela B. Tanguay
Foreword by Sue Thompson
ISBN 978 1 85302 941 7

of related interest

Asperger's Syndrome
A Guide for Parents and Professionals
Tony Attwood
Foreword by Lorna Wing
ISBN 978 1 85302 577 8

Stepping Out
Using Games and Activities to Help Your Child with Special Needs
Sarah Newman
ISBN 978 1 84310 110 9

Relationship Development Intervention with Young Children
Social and Emotional Development Activities for Asperger Syndrome, Autism, PDD and NLD
Steven E. Gutstein and Rachelle K. Sheely
ISBN 978 1 84310 714 0

A Special Kind of Brain
Living with Nonverbal Learning Disability
Nancy Burger
Foreword by Byron P Rourke
ISBN 978 1 84310 762 0

Raising NLD Superstars
What Families with Nonverbal Learning Disabilities Need to Know about
Marcia Brown Rubinstien
ISBN 978 1 84310 770 5

Nonverbal Learning Disabilities at Home
A Parent's Guide

Pamela B. Tanguay

Foreword by Byron P. Rourke, FRSC

Jessica Kingsley Publishers
London and Philadelphia

First published in the United Kingdom in 2001
by Jessica Kingsley Publishers
73 Collier Street
London N1 9BE, UK
and
400 Market Street, Suite 400
Philadelphia, PA 19106, USA

www.jkp.com

Library of Congress Cataloging in Publication Data

Tanguay, Pamela B., 1947–
    Nonverbal learning disabilities at home : a parent's guide / Pamela B. Tanguay.
        p. cm.
    Includes bibliographical references and index.
    ISBN 1-85302-940-8
        1. Learning disabled children--Unites States--Life skills guides. 2. Learning disabled children--Home care--United States. 3. Social skills in children--United States. 4. Parents of handicapped children--United States. I. Title.

HV894 .T38 2001
649'.152--dc21

00-048387

British Library Cataloguing in Publication Data
A CIP catalogue record for this book is available from the British Library

ISBN 978 1 85302 940 0

Printed and bound in the United States by Thomson-Shore, Inc.

Contents

Acknowledgements

During my journey to understanding Nonverbal Learning Disabilities (NLD), I've made several special friends. First, there was Joan Scott, my partner in the development of *NLD on the Web!* and sounding board on so many topics and projects, not the least of which was this book. Barb Kirby came next as I researched the similarities between NLD and Asperger's syndrome, who then introduced me to Rhona Silver and Echo Fling, also members of the Asperger's community. And finally, there is Liane Willey who is the ultimate role model for my daughter. All have become dear to me, and share the same journey as we raise our children. Thank you all for being such special individuals. We're fortunate to have each other.

Over the years, we have worked with dozens of professionals. However, there is one in particular whom I would like to acknowledge. Dr. Julia Ramos Grenier, our neuropsychologist of ten years, introduced my husband and I to the world of NLD, badgered me when I was stubborn, and fought alongside us for our daughter when the educational monster invariably reared its ugly head. She also reviewed the first chapter of this book for accuracy. For all of your help, I am extremely grateful.

To Dr. Byron Rourke for his decades of NLD research, and Sue Thompson for her mission to educate the educators, a heartfelt thank you. Without your dedication, our children's futures would be far less promising.

Finally, a thank you to my sister Linda Mayberry for her feedback and suggestions for improving this book. To my husband Ray, who read several versions of this book, provided both a parental and analytical perspective, and reassured me as my confidence faltered, what would I do without you? From the bottom of my heart, thank you for being my best friend, for sharing your life with me, and for giving me the special gift of our daughter…

This book, the work which preceded it, and that which will certainly follow, is dedicated to my daughter Stef who brings out the best in me. You are a treasure, sweetheart, and I love you with all my heart.

Mom

Foreword

Providing efficacious intervention/therapeutic programs for children and adolescents who exhibit the syndrome of Nonverbal Learning Disabilities (NLD) is a complicated undertaking. First, there is the necessity to understand the content (neuropsychological assets and deficits) of those who exhibit the syndrome. Second, there is the task of determining the developmental dynamics within which it has emerged. Third, there are the therapeutic decisions that must be made regarding such issues as the capacity of caregivers to deliver the program, idiosyncrasies of the child/adolescent that may enhance or impede the implementation of the program, and a host of other dimensions that relate specifically to the current milieu (including its therapeutic capacities and deficiencies) in which the person with NLD is developing. And finally, there is the daunting task of proffering efficacious, concrete, therapeutic suggestions for the myriad of day-to-day problems that persons with NLD face.

The reader of this book will soon realize that all of these requirements are part and parcel of it. And that these are melded into a framework that is not only eminently reasonable, but very readable.

The author is to be commended for bringing the fruits of her research into the origins and developmental course of NLD to this undertaking. She is also to be congratulated for taking on the complex task of formulating and testing methods of intervention that make sense theoretically and that, for the most part, can be applied in a systematic manner by most persons with no extensive background in the helping professions.

What is required of the caregiver (at what we may refer to as a 'working' level) is the capacity to examine carefully and apply prudently the suggestions spread within the book. What is required at a very different level is the motivation and stamina to continue to pursue efficacious interventions even when these proceed in a painfully slow manner or when setbacks occur. What is required at a related level is the capacity to countenance and put into perspective real or imagined failures in the attainment of targeted adaptive skills for the sake of the long-term benefit of the child.

There is nothing in this work that would suggest that intervention for the child or adolescent with NLD is easy. That said, there is a wealth of material that, in the hands of a sensitive and concerned caregiver, can be applied in a fairly straightforward manner and evaluated in terms of its efficacy for the youngster in question.

The author has provided a book that is essential reading for caregivers of children and adolescents with NLD. It should not only be read but kept on hand for easy reference as the youngster develops. It should be valued as a rich source of helpful suggestions, and as a springboard for the creativity of the concerned caregiver.

Pamela Tanguay has done all of us involved with the syndrome of NLD a great favor by providing this book.

Byron P. Rourke, FRSC
September 2000

Introduction

NLD is by definition a syndrome, consisting of a cluster of assets and deficits. Although the neuropsychological pattern is present in each person, the mix of strengths and weaknesses comes together uniquely in each child. Some children may be more physically awkward, while others may have more social deficits, and others still may have significant impairment in all deficit areas of the syndrome. Another variable is the age of the NLD child. A youngster in first grade may appear more capable than when they reach adolescence. And finally, a child with an exceptionally high IQ may be able to compensate somewhat better than a child of average intelligence. Clearly, NLD is not a 'cookie cutter' disability where the individual looks the same from youth to adulthood, and where the syndrome appears in the same way from individual to individual.

The primary purpose of this book is to present the problems NLD children may face in their everyday life, as well as suggesting strategies for helping them cope and grow. To that end, each area of deficit is portrayed as a significant impairment. Although some children may in fact fit this profile, many others will not.

This book specifically addresses NLD children from preschool through adolescence. However, older teens and even young adults may benefit from much of the content. Please keep in mind that this book is not meant to be a blueprint for 'fixing' NLD. It was written to simplify the description of the difficulties faced by individuals with the disorder, illustrate how it may present in everyday activities, and outline strategies which could benefit such. I hope it will be a springboard to help you develop an intervention program specific to the needs of your child and family.

The strategies outlined within this book may serve a broad audience. There are many children who have NLD, either alone, or as part of a medical or psychiatric condition. Some of the medical conditions which result in NLD are Williams, Velocardiofacial and de Lange syndromes, Callosal agenesis, hydrocephalus and others. Disorders which often share the NLD learning profile include Asperger's syndrome and Pervasive Developmental Disorder – Not Otherwise Specified (PDD–NOS) (Rourke 1995).[1] Any child who has a neuropsychological profile of NLD will benefit from the material contained within this book.

While writing this book, I have taken editorial license in two areas. The first is gender reference. Today, the politically correct way to address gender is to alternate between the use of male and female. However, since this work is dedicated to my daughter, I chose to use the female gender throughout the book. The second issue also relates to politcal correctness. You will note that I use the phrase 'NLD child or children.' Some people prefer the phrase 'child with NLD' because they believe that it is more appropriate to put the child before the disability, rather than characterize the child by their disability. I think that this is a fair point. However, the use of 'NLD child' seems less stilted and more personal than 'child with NLD.' I hope that I do not offend anyone by my choices.

Since I live with NLD every day, as my daughter struggles with its many challenges, this book was written with a piece of my heart on every page. I hope that you enjoy it, but more important, that you find it helpful. If you do, then watch for its companion volume for teachers, *Nonverbal Learning Disabilities: At School*, to be released in the spring of 2002.

Pamela B. Tanguay

---

1   Please read *Syndrome of Nonverbal Learning Disabilities: Neurodevelopmental Manifestations*, edited by Byron P. Rourke, for a full explanation of the disorders, diseases and dysfunction which result in NLD. Additional information on this book can be found in the Annotated Bibliography included in the appendices at the back of this book.

Chapter 1

NLD – What Is It?

The term Nonverbal Learning Disabilities (NLD) can be quite confusing. At first blush, you might think that individuals with this disability are nonverbal. Just the opposite – these kids may actually talk your ear off. Nonverbal Learning Disabilities means that the primary areas of deficit are in the *nonverbal* domains. NLD is considered a syndrome, meaning that the disability is comprised of a cluster of skill deficits which impact virtually every aspect of the individual's life. As a result of the pervasive implications of NLD, it is a serious and sometimes profound disability. Rather than think of the disorder as a learning disability in the traditional sense, it may be more helpful to consider it in terms of a developmental disability.

The definition of a developmental disability is quite global in nature. It assumes a severe, chronic disability which is present before the individual reaches the age of 21. It further assumes substantial functional limitation in areas such as self-care, receptive and expressive language, learning, self-direction, and mobility, as well as the capacity for independent living and economic self-sufficiency. This definition is certainly a closer description of the implications of NLD than what we generally understand a learning disability to be.

Our traditional understanding of a learning disability is much narrower in scope (for example, dyslexia), and is considered as primarily affecting academic learning. NLD, on the other hand, affects the individual's ability to learn academic *and* life skills.

In order to provide appropriate intervention for the NLD child, it is important to understand the global nature of the disorder. When first hearing the term learning disability, many parents may initially believe that the problem should properly be addressed within the school setting. Although the academic issues are the responsibility of the school district, there are other functional limitations which must be addressed. To what extent these will be handled by school personnel will depend on the individual child's needs and how willing the district is to cooperate. However, with even the broadest school support, there are many areas of intervention which will fall to the parents. This book will address those issues.

Much of the available literature describing NLD is technical in nature, and may be difficult for parents and caregivers to understand. If your child has been identified as having NLD, and/or you have researched this disorder, you have encountered terms such as social-emotional and adaptational deficits, tactile difficulties, psychomotor coordination problems, and so on. Although these are some of the inherent deficits of the disability, throughout this book we will attempt to use more 'user-friendly' terminology.

STRENGTHS AND WEAKNESSES

The primary strengths of NLD children are auditory and verbal. Most will develop a sophisticated vocabulary before they enter school, often well beyond that of their peers. Generally they have excellent attention and memory for what they hear, unless the material is complex. These strengths may not be as noticeable in younger NLD children, but will become more obvious as they

this is why Kenji says he loves Daniel! He said Daniel is the only boy he can actually have a conversation with –

mature. By the time that they reach the upper elementary and middle school grades, it should be apparent that they are auditory learners.

Although each individual is unique, children with NLD will have varying degrees of difficulty in the following areas.

Tactile (touch) and visual attention *and* perception

[handwritten margin note: → doesn't know where he is full]

She may be unable to process correctly what she touches or sees, with poor attention for both. For example, the child may be unable to identify something familiar by touching or holding it, or recognize her house by appearance alone.

Psychomotor coordination (physical awkwardness)

The child may have difficulty getting her body to do what she wants it to, when she wants it to, and how she wants it to. For example, hopping, skipping, jumping, catching and throwing a ball, or riding a bicycle are all psychomotor coordination activities which are likely to be a challenge.

Adaptability

[handwritten star marks] She will almost certainly have considerable difficulty adapting to changes in her established routine. The child does not have the ability to 'wing it.' For example, if the child is at the sitter's, and you will be picking her up late, you might ask the sitter to put her in her pajamas so that she is ready for bed when you pick her up. However, the NLD child will be totally confused by this change in her routine, because she always puts her pajamas on in her own bedroom right before going to bed in her own bed.

[handwritten margin notes: – substitutes at school – field trips at school – new restaurants – babysitters – member Brittany when babysat during Tricia's wedding ?]

Spatial orientation

She will be likely to have significant difficulty knowing where she is, or where other objects are, in space. For example, she may miscalculate how close she is to a lamp, and inadvertently knock it over, or gauge a door opening incorrectly, and bump into the door jamb. *– spilling drinks etc.*

Mental flexibility

The child learns and thinks very concretely, and processes information in a black-and-white manner, not understanding shades of gray. She thinks in concrete, logical terms. Abstract concepts are often beyond the child's ability. In all likelihood, she will do poorly with open-ended questions. For example, if asked, 'How was your day?' she may not have a response. There are too many variables in the question of 'how,' and since she can't figure out what you mean, she won't answer. However, if asked a concrete question such as 'Did you have your spelling test today?' she can respond, because she has a clear understanding of what is being asked.

Executive function and organization

She will have difficulty prioritizing and organizing both her thoughts and her work. For example, if the child is given a large assignment in school, she will not be able to break it down into its component parts, or determine the sequence of tasks – which task must be completed before another can be accomplished.

Pragmatics of language

Pragmatic language is the functional use of language. These children cannot 'read between the lines' or interpret other nonverbal communication. Although she may have a well developed vocabulary, there will probably be significant communication difficulties because her expressive and receptive language is based only on words. For example, if you say 'I have to run to the grocery store,' the neurologically typical (NT) child will know that 'run' is a figure of speech. The NLD child might say 'But mom, why aren't you going to take the car?'

Generalizing information

The NLD child is unable to apply prior learned knowledge to a new but similar topic or situation. For example, when learning about the Presidents of the US, and who served in what order, the NLD child will memorize the information that William Jefferson Clinton is the forty-second President. If a test question is 'Who won the most recent Presidential election?' the child may draw a blank, even though to most students the question seems easy. If the information which the child has stored is different than the way it is asked on a test, the child will be unable to make the connection between the two facts, or reorganize and 'generalize' the information.

he tried to do this with candy spray. "Ms Silva gives stuff back at end of the day...")

Social skills

Difficulties with pragmatics, inference and generalization result in pronounced social problems. The child does not understand our culture, or the social rules governing appropriate behavior. For example, at a birthday party, or a school dance, the NLD child may seem disruptive, and act in a very immature way. If you are on vacation, and suggest to such children that they might want to bring gifts back for their classmates, the response may be 'Why should I do that? Nobody asked me to bring them anything.'

Emotional stability

Owing to the child's inability to order her world, adapt to new situations, and comprehend nonverbal messages such as voice inflection, body language and so forth, she may be riddled with anxiety which may increase with age as her environment becomes more complex. For example, the young NLD child may cry often when at school, or seem confused much of the time. The adolescent may become quite withdrawn and depressed as academic and social demands increase.

WHAT CAUSES NLD?

Dr. Byron P. Rourke of the University of Windsor in Canada and Yale University in Connecticut is the preeminent researcher in the field of Nonverbal Learning Disabilities. After decades of research, Dr. Rourke and his associates have determined that the disorder is caused by damage to white matter in the brain (Rourke 1989, 1995).

A very simplistic definition of white matter is that it is brain tissue made up of nerve cells which connect various parts of the brain to each other. It is called white matter because the nerve fibers are coated with myelin, a light-colored fatty substance which acts as insulation. In essence, it is the brain's wiring system. The myelin sheath can be compared to the plastic coating we find on electrical wires, and allows for rapid and accurate transmission of information within the brain. If the myelin sheath is damaged (as Dr. Rourke indicates may be the case with NLD), the child's processing speed is reduced, and the signal may not be sent accurately, or arrive at the proper destination. Therefore, although the information centers within the brain may be intact, the transmission of signals is not working properly. In other words, there is a 'short circuit' somewhere in the child's brain. Information about the brain tells us that there is a disproportionate amount of white matter in the right hemisphere of the brain compared to the left. Therefore the disability is sometimes referred to as Right Hemisphere Syndrome, meaning that the right hemisphere is dysfunctional because of white-matter damage.

[handwritten margin note, right side:] unclear, is the decision than processing

[handwritten note, bottom:] when you process something you are reviewing info and then making a decision as to how to act. If you have trouble

In contrast, it appears that function in the left hemisphere remains relatively intact. Therefore, language, step-by-step reasoning, and other skills which are processed by the left hemisphere are more preserved. The right hemisphere, dealing with spatial, abstract, intuitive and other 'nonverbal' aspects, is impaired. Also, since higher-order thinking skills require the use of both hemispheres to integrate complex information, these skills are also impaired because one of the hemispheres isn't working properly.

For a more thorough understanding of Dr. Rourke's research into white matter dysfunction and Nonverbal Learning Disabilities, there are two books in particular that you will find helpful: *Nonverbal Learning Disabilities, The Syndrome and the Model,* and *Syndrome of Nonverbal Learning Disabilities, Neurodevelopmental Manifestations.* Information on both of these books is included in Appendix II at the end of this book.

NLD IS OFTEN MISDIAGNOSED

Unfortunately, due to limited awareness of NLD, many children, especially when they are young, are misdiagnosed. Because of their poor planning and organizational skills, their apparent problems with impulse control and their inability to attend to tactile (touch) and visual information, educators often misdiagnose NLD children as having Attention Deficit Disorder (ADD) or Attention Deficit/Hyperactivity Disorder (AD/HD). Keep in mind that tactile and visual modalities are probably the most commonly used educational strategies in the first few years of school. These are areas of deficit for NLD children who would naturally appear to be unable to 'attend' to tactile and/or visual material.

Another common misdiagnosis within the NLD population is anxiety or panic disorder. It is true that many of these children have very high levels of anxiety, however their anxiety is actually the result of their disability – NLD.

BRIGHT AND LEARNING DISABLED

If your child is young, say five to eight years old, it may be difficult for you to comprehend the magnitude of this disability, and how significantly it will affect her in just a few short years. Although you will see problems in the young child that are disturbing – her inability to button buttons, zip zippers, put on a T-shirt, use eating utensils effectively – you also see that she is bright, articulate and engaging, particularly with adults. Since she is so bright, articulate and engaging, how can there be a problem? Like the parents and caregivers, the teacher sees an inquisitive child, with an excellent vocabulary, who reads well (although some NLD children have early reading difficulties), spells well and learns basic math facts. Although the child's handwriting may be poor, that is not unusual for students in their early school years. The child's social skills appear immature, but that is also not unusual for this age group. Clearly, because of the child's obvious verbal strengths, it is difficult for parents, caregivers and teachers to grasp how sig-nificant the disability is while the child is young.

To make matters worse, the verbal strengths of the child, coupled with the appearance of academic competence may present a false illusion of giftedness. At this stage, it may be particularly difficult for a teacher to appreciate that NLD is a debilitating disorder, whose full impact may not be realized until the child is nine, ten, or eleven years old. It has been said that this is a disability that a child 'grows into,' which makes a certain amount of sense. The skill deficits of these individuals are not seriously challenged until the upper elementary grades, when teaching begins to move away from the child's areas of strength – simple rote memory, vocabulary, spelling and single-word decoding skills. As academic challenges increase, and the child can no longer depend on her compensatory skills, difficulties in school and at home become apparent. As is often the case with children having learning difficulties, the first sign may be the child's anger and frustration. It will take a skilled clinician to properly evaluate and diagnose NLD.

INTERVENTION IS CRITICAL

Understanding NLD and its implications is the key to appropriate intervention. It is a very serious disability, but there are excellent prospects for the child if it is identified early and interventions are provided appropriately. These children can be taught just about anything. However, the operative word here is 'taught.' Such children will not learn through observation, assimilating information along the way. They must be taught everything explicitly, in a verbal, scripted, step-by-step manner. An example here may be helpful.

Your NLD child might not know how to do simple, everyday tasks. We don't generally have to consciously teach our children how to do things such as open a door or window. Neurologically typical children seem to grasp these common everyday tasks intuitively, sometimes much sooner than we realize. How many parents find that toddlers have let themselves outside, while the parent frantically searches the house for them? You won't often find this problem with an NLD child who probably finds opening a door or window a complete mystery. For these children, you must directly teach these 'simple' tasks. Teaching them to open a window in your home might go something like this: you would say, letting the child accomplish each step before going on to the next, 'Pull up the blinds by pulling down on the cord on the right hand side of the blinds…unlock the window by pushing that latch at the top to the right…now push the window up towards the ceiling.'

If the child is later faced with a window that cranks out, rather than pushes up, she will have to be taught that task as if it were new, because to her, it is. Remember, she doesn't generalize information, and her nonverbal problem solving skills are deficient. So, once again, you would teach the child the task by verbally scripting each step in the order that it is to be done.

NLD children are often bright kids, and some are very bright. They have a different learning style, and need to be taught in a verbally scripted manner. When taught to her learning style, the child may grasp some things quite quickly, often only needing to have new material explained once. At other times, she may need repetition. With our neurologically typical children, we aren't consciously aware of how often they watch us perform a task before they learn how to do it. At some point, we just realize that they have figured it out on their own. It probably didn't take any specific work on our part to teach them, but with the NLD child it will. Initially, having to consciously and explicitly teach them everything will likely feel unnatural. However, as you see your child begin to grasp what you teach her, it will become more comfortable and natural to you.

SUMMARY

NLD is a pervasive, neurologically based learning disability which is caused by damage to the brain's circuitry. It results in significant deficits which are remediated through the child's auditory and verbal strengths, in a step-by-step manner.

Areas of deficit

- *Tactile (touch) perception* – the ability to identify something by touch alone;

- *Tactile (touch) attention* – the ability to 'attend' to teaching strategies that require touch;

- *Visual perception* – the ability to accurately scan the visual field or environment and process what is seen;

- *Visual attention* – the ability to 'attend' to teaching strategies that use the visual modality;

- *Spatial orientation* – the awareness of where an individual is in space and their physical proximity to other objects;

- *Psychomotor Coordination* – the ability to have your body do what you want it to, when you want it to, how you want it to;

- *Generalizing information* – the application of prior learned information to a similar situation;

SUMMARY

- *Mental flexibility* – the ability to assimilate and process new information or ideas that may influence the way that you think about a topic or situation;

- *Pragmatics* – the functional and practical use of language;

- *Social skills* – the ability to interact appropriately, based on established social norms;

- *Adaptability* – the capacity to adjust to a new situation or change in circumstances;

- *Emotional stability* – consistency in emotional well-being;

- *Executive function and organization* – the ability to organize, prioritize and plan thoughts and work.

Chapter 2

Early Warning Signs

Although NLD is often not diagnosed until a child is at least eight years old, looking back, there were early warning signs if we parents and our children's pediatricians knew what to look for.

Many of us saw these early signs, but either thought that our child just had their own unique course of development, or were reassured by a pediatrician who said that all children are different, and not to worry. When we asked about our child's progress toward developmental milestones, we were told that developmental milestones, as outlined in baby books, are simply guidelines, and again, not to worry. When you think back to those early days, do you recall any of the following?

○ Did your child have difficulty calming down, even as early as infancy? Did she have the ability to self-soothe, that is, could she calm down without your assistance?

○ Did your child have sleep difficulties? Were you aware that prolonged sleep disturbances really aren't typical, and are often one sign of a developmental disability?

○ Was your child a very agreeable toddler? Did she quietly play on a blanket rather than crawling all over the room? Did you watch other parents chasing after their toddlers, and think how fortunate you were? Were you aware of the importance of motor activity to the normal development of your child? Did you have any idea that a lack of motoric activity might create major developmental difficulties for your child later on?

○ Did your child have recurring hiccups as an infant? Were you aware that hiccups in an infant are often an indication of agitation or stress?

Why would a parent be alarmed if their baby has the hiccups, doesn't sleep well, is fussy, and as a toddler isn't the terror of the neighborhood? The fact is that they probably wouldn't, although these are some of the things you might see with an NLD infant or toddler. But there is more.

MISSED CUES

At six to nine months of age, the neurologically typical (NT) child is fascinated by new places, things and people. A trip to the supermarket is likely to be an exciting adventure for her. She grabs at the colorful packages, smiles at the passers-by, and wiggles all over when someone tries to engage her. Not so for the NLD child, who may be terrified as you enter a store, her eyes as wide as saucers. Although at first glance, she may appear to be curiously looking around, on closer observation it may be fear that you see on her little face.

When the pediatrician finally said it was time to introduce your baby to solid foods, you probably made a beeline for the supermarket. You loaded your shopping cart with lots of goodies – little jars of meat, vegetables, fruit, and so on.

When it is time for baby's first meal of solid food, you seat yourself in front of her for the big moment – 'Yum, yum, you'll *like* green beans!' Your little one opens her mouth like a baby bird, takes the first mouthful, and promptly gags. Okay, it's new you think, let's try some sweet potatoes and see how that goes. Success – she loves it! However, the cycle continues – she eats some fruits, few

[handwritten margin note: Daniel used to cru? be agitated]

vegetables, no meat, and you mentally write it off to having a picky eater.

You are pleased, however, that your baby always wants her hands wiped. As she eats finger foods, she holds out her hands between bites to be cleaned off; you swell with pride at having such a neat baby. When you begin teaching her how to hold and use a spoon, she doesn't seem to 'get it,' but you keep trying, and she persists with using her fingers, and having them wiped off between bites. Baby wipes are now a mainstay of the kitchen table as well as the changing table.

As your baby's first birthday approaches, you and your family plan the perfect party. All the relatives will be there – grandparents, aunts, uncles, and cousins, as well as close friends. The house is decorated, and you make, or order, that special cake to celebrate the occasion. The day arrives, and you dress your baby in one of those adorable outfits that have yet to be worn. She immediately starts tugging at her clothes and fussing, but in all of the excitement you miss the signal. The doorbell rings as guests arrive, cameras are everywhere, and all are having a great time – except the guest of honor, who is utterly overwhelmed. At some point between the arrival of the first guest, opening presents, and singing happy birthday as the cake is presented, the baby disintegrates. What started as fussiness, escalates to a howl. Relatives say, 'Oh the poor thing, she must be tired/hungry/need a diaper change,' and do not realize that the child needs to be removed from the chaos.

These examples may not relate specifically to your child, but you'll recall others. Parents naturally adapt to the idiosyncrasies of their children, and their apparently unique characteristics. As long as they are subtle, these traits are just considered to be part of their child's personality. However, as NLD children move through the toddler period, more obvious manifestations of their differences begin to surface.

ADDITIONAL WARNING SIGNS

You begin to notice that you don't see the extent of facial expression or interaction that you expected. Although you may have accepted that your child is quiet and shy, it seems to be more than that. Where other children of the same age are gurgling, cooing, and trying valiantly to gain *anyone's* attention, the NLD baby is quietly passive.

And then there are those other little signs:

- She doesn't seem to learn cause and effect – for example, if she climbs up on something, there is a danger of falling and getting hurt. Even when she does fall and get hurt, she doesn't seem to learn from the experience, but will repeat the activity, once again falling and being hurt.

- She may have excessive fears – of the vacuum cleaner, lawnmower, washing machine, animals, and the dark.

- Her initial attempts at walking may be unsteady. Although all toddlers appear unsteady at first, NLD children are more awkward, and for a longer period of time. However, parents easily miss this distinction between neurologically typical toddlers and NLD toddlers, especially if this is their first child.

[handwritten margin note: no — but no crawling — hated even trying.]

- Walking up and down stairs may continue to be one step at a time for longer than anticipated, or the child may choose not to walk on the stairs at all, but may go up or down on their little bottom instead.

- In all likelihood, the child hates surprises, and startles easily. This is not a child who is entertained by you popping up from behind a couch and saying, 'Boo!' While the neurologically typical child gleefully giggles, the NLD child may howl in fright.

° These children clearly respond quite poorly to changes to their routine. Same old, same old, is not boring to her. For the NLD child, consistency provides security.

And of course there are the social issues. As you introduce your little one to a playgroup, or simply to another friend's child, she doesn't respond the way you would expect. She is late to parallel play (two toddlers playing side-by-side), and later still to engage another child in a play activity. In all likelihood, when she does engage, it is inappropriate, or a bit 'off.'

IDENTIFICATION IN YOUNG CHILDREN

Looking back, you can recall your own list of disquieting concerns. Although the warning signs of NLD in small children are subtle, your child's doctor should not have ignored the early warning signs that something was amiss. Pediatricians need to be more attuned to developmental deviations, no matter how minor they appear to be, and then monitor the child carefully and/or refer them to a specialist who is more familiar with the nuances of child development.

If your child is young, and you are questioning her development, there are now pediatricians who specialize specifically in developmental disabilities. They are called developmental pediatricians, and work in a fairly new field within the medical profession. There are several ways to locate these specialists. The first, and most obvious, is to look in the physician specialties section of the phone book under the heading of developmental pediatricians. You can also contact a pediatric neurologist, or the department of pediatrics or developmental disabilities at an area hospital, any of which should know if there is a developmental pediatrician in the area. Another option is to contact the children's hospital which services your area, since there may well be a developmental pediatrician on staff.

Although it would be ideal for NLD youngsters to be recognized when they are still toddlers, it is more likely that they will be identified later, probably around age eight or older. Regardless of when the child is diagnosed, intervention increases the likelihood of a successful long-term prognosis. However, the older the child, the more difficult the intervention will be. To put it another way, early is better, but later is not hopeless.

SUMMARY

There are many subtle early warning indicators of Non-verbal Learning Disabilities. Parents should trust their instincts if they feel that their child is not developing normally, regardless of what other well-intentioned individuals might say to them. If the child's doctor is not responsive to the parent's concerns, it is wise to pursue the issue with a different medical professional. Developmental pediatricians specialize in the evaluation and care of children with developmental delays, disorders, and disabilities and would probably be the most capable of determining whether there was something atypical in your child's development.

- trouble eating - lots of spit up - ate too much, too fast than threw it up - tried multiple formulas

- trouble sleeping - not a baby who could cry himself to sleep - used to take hours! I had to get a book and follow the steps . . . .

Chapter 3

The Parent's Role

As you have already read, NLD is not a learning disability in the traditional sense. The neurological impairments that these children have affect virtually every aspect of their life. It is not a problem which can or should be dealt with exclusively in the school environment, or by classroom teachers, although they should play a significant role in the child's intervention program.

As the parent of an impaired child, you will be wearing many hats that you might not have anticipated – parent yes, but also facilitator, translator, tutor, and coach. Although there are various professionals who can be of tremendous assistance – such as speech and language specialists, occupational therapists and physical therapists – you may not have access to all or any of these services. Whether you do or don't, *you* will play the pivotal role in your child's development.

In Chapter 1, you read that this child will need direct instruction in every aspect of her life. Much of that learning process occurs within the home and family. She will need instruction in all of the areas typical of raising a child, from dressing, personal hygiene and manners, to how to get home from her friend's house. The key difference with the NLD child is that the instruction needs to be step-by-step, and learning may take considerably longer than for a neurologically typical child.

PARENT TRAPS

There are some very real human emotions that may derail your efforts in helping your child. If you are in denial, or haven't yet fully accepted the scope of your child's disability, you won't be able to provide the appropriate, and necessary, ongoing intervention. It is natural and important to grieve when you realize that your child will be faced with lifelong challenges. Grieving is part of the acceptance process which needs to occur before you can effectively help your child overcome or compensate for her NLD. Much of the literature on the long-term prognosis for individuals with Nonverbal Learning Disabilities is discouraging. However, much of that same literature is based on individuals who did not receive intervention as children. Don't adopt an attitude of defeat – acknowledge the challenge, and then do everything in your power to help your child to reach her fullest potential.

The second parenting trap that you should avoid is the temptation to do for your child those things that are difficult for her. Teach her, yes. Help her, yes. But, don't continue to do for her those things that she has learned to do for herself. If you fall prey to this protective instinct, you will hurt rather than help your child.

There is a condition called 'learned helplessness,' unwittingly created by parents and caregivers who do so much for a child that she actually becomes helpless, and can't (or doesn't believe that she can), do anything for herself. You do not want to head down that road. In addition to fostering dependence, you also run the very distinct risk of creating a sibling resentment problem if you have other children. A neurologically typical child will quickly identify a double standard if one exists, and resentment of the NLD child is almost a certainty. Chores should be given to both or all children, with assigned tasks commensurate with their respective abilities.

As parents, we raise our children with the intent that they will become self-sufficient adults, and it should be no different for your NLD child. Although she has a serious disability, she needn't become crippled by it. She needs to be *taught* to do things for herself – using a supportive, nurturing approach when she is young – gradually withdrawing assistance as she grows and masters tasks. Although the temptation to create a cocoon around your child may be powerful, it is critical that you resist the urge. Although these children *do* need to be protected from the very real dangers they face, both physical and emotional, you'll need to strike a balance between protector and coach.

THE PARENT AND INTERVENTION

Whether you are directly providing intervention for your child, or working with a professional who is, it is absolutely imperative that you be involved in the process. No one will ever know your child as well as you do. This child's needs and issues are often quite subtle, and only readily apparent to the immediate family. As her parent, you will know where she should and shouldn't be prodded and when she is ready to take on new challenges, as well as when she is overwhelmed. If a professional is working with your child, you will need to provide this perspective.

You will also need to continue the learning process at home that is initiated by a professional. The more consistently the task is reinforced, the more likely it is that the child will master it. For instance, if you are fortunate enough to have an occupational therapist (OT) working with your child to teach her self-help skills, they may be teaching her how to put a button through a buttonhole. If you continue to button the child's clothes for her at home, rather than reinforce what the therapist is doing, it will undermine the learning process. Or, worse yet, the child may believe that she doesn't have to do things for herself at home. It is important to work with the therapist as a partner, with both of you working toward the same goal.

Although many NLD children are not diagnosed until they are at least eight years old, here's hoping that you are one of the fortunate ones who have an early diagnosis. The remainder of this book will cover things that you can do to help your child develop skills in many different areas. If your child is older, it would still be beneficial to read the information which pertains to the younger years. You may find that you have intuitively intervened quite effectively, or that something that went unnoticed is currently causing difficulty for your child. Also, the purpose of this book is to encourage you to think creatively, and develop interventions for your child's particular needs. It is not intended to provide a parenting 'blueprint' for raising an NLD child. If you read all of the sections, even those that may pertain to a younger age, you may be able to modify a suggestion so that it applies to your older child. I hope that, after reading this book, you will be able to develop a unique intervention approach which works for your child and family.

THE PARENT AS FACILITATOR

One of the most important roles you can play for your child is that of facilitator. NLD children want desperately to understand what is expected of them, and to fit in. However, they don't understand our language or our culture. Yes, they probably have a great vocabulary, and may sound quite articulate. But just because they have a strong vocabulary, that doesn't mean that they are able to use language functionally. We communicate in many ways, and the majority of them are nonverbal. A gesture, a tone of voice, or a facial expression sends a message, but for these children, the message is hidden. We use sarcasm to make a point, but sarcasm is lost on these children, and may actually be cruel. We intuit what someone means, even if it isn't what they say. NLD children depend on words alone, and then only when the words are used in a predictable way. They want you to say what you mean, and mean what you say. Words with multiple meanings will be likely to throw them off stride.

If you have ever studied a foreign language in school, and then tried to speak it with natives of a foreign country, you may be close to understanding what it is like for the NLD child. Natives use colloquial expressions that you don't learn in a classroom. However, beyond the spoken word, you have an additional skill that the NLD child doesn't. You can revert to nonverbal means to communicate when words alone fail, while NLD children can't. No matter how sophisticated a person's vocabulary, words alone won't allow for effective communication.

Words alone comprise a mere 35%, or less, of communication. The remaining 65%, or more, is nonverbal, such as facial expression, tone of voice, body language, etc. Words are actually a secondary, rather than a primary form of communication. Therefore, the NLD child often misses the majority of the intended message in social interaction. Unfortunately, all too often, adults have the erroneous impression that the child's strong vocabulary automatically makes her a good communicator. This is definitely *not* true! You will need to be your child's translator, making sure that she understands language, both verbal *and* nonverbal. There is a complete chapter dedicated to communication skills later in this book.

THE PARENT AS SOCIAL COACH

All cultures have social 'rules,' and most of us learn them without even being consciously aware of it. We learn very early that what we may say to our friends is not something that we would say to our teacher. These are the unwritten guidelines that allow us to function effectively in society. NLD children won't have this knowledge unless they are specifically taught. Don't expect your child to assimilate this type of information on her own. You will need to provide social scripts for her, and explain the 'rules' to her so that she understands what is expected.

Let's return to our analogy of being in a foreign country. If you found yourself in India, and didn't understand the language or culture, you would be totally and completely lost. Your nonverbal skills might actually create additional communication problems, because symbolic gestures may have an offensive meaning in India. You would have to find someone who could act as your interpreter – someone who understands both the language and the culture. NLD children are constantly lost, confused, and overwhelmed. Just as you would make social blunders in an unfamiliar country, they make similar mistakes every day, without a clue as to what they did wrong. Just as you would quickly become frustrated in India, it is no wonder we often see what we perceive as behavior problems with NLD youngsters.

Although the child may get angry for no apparent reason, it is quite likely that there is a very specific reason that she acts out. In most cases, you will find that it is a misunderstanding. The child may have misunderstood what was said, what was meant, or the rules governing a particular social situation. It is important to know what caused the problem in order to teach her the skills that may help her prevent the same difficulty from happening again. As with communication, there is an entire chapter dedicated to social skills later in this book.

THE PARENT AS ADVOCATE

Once your child is in school, you will take on the additional role of being her advocate. It is very likely that the school has never heard of NLD, and will either not know how to support her, or oppose your request for intervention. Remember, they see a bright, verbally articulate student who projects an illusion of competency. They are far more familiar with left hemisphere reading disorders, such as decoding problems, which are very apparent. Since our educational system prizes language skills, and even the young NLD child seems to possess more than is common for her age, their reaction might well be, 'what problem?' It will become your job to ensure that your child is receiving the appropriate services to which the law entitles her. As part of your role as advocate, you will need to become conversant with the legislation governing education and disabilities. A daunting task!

THE PARENT AS CAREGIVER

In a two-parent household, your child will probably connect with one parent more than the other. Typically, the parent who spends more time with the NLD child is more familiar with her needs, and knows when she is overwhelmed. Generally, this is the primary caregiver, so it is often the mother. Whichever parent it is, it is not a simple preference on the part of the child, but rather a strong dependence. The child looks to the favored parent as their 'translator' – the person who interprets the mystifying world around them, and the culture that the child doesn't understand. The parent who is not the primary caregiver should not abdicate his or her parental responsibility. It is the responsibility of *both* parents to be involved in the parenting of the NLD child.

Teaching this child is an exhausting process, and requires constant work. The primary caregiver will become overwhelmed if the full responsibility falls to them. Just as you must guard against sibling rivalry, you must also guard against resentment building within your relationship. The parent who is not the primary caregiver must do two things – be an involved parent, under-standing the issues of the NLD child, and provide support and respite to the primary caregiving parent. You must act as a team, each making your own specific and unique contributions to the parenting process.

Let's consider what an evening at home might look like. Let's assume that Dad works outside of the home, and Mom is the primary caregiver for two children, one with NLD and the other who is NT. It's homework time, and the NLD child is exhausted and begins to cling to Mom. Dad thinks that mom is better able to deal with the NLD child, and decides he will help the NT child with his homework. Although it may be true that Mom is better able to deal with the NLD child, unless Dad becomes more involved, the responsibility for the NLD child will continue to fall to Mom. However, Mom is also exhausted, and needs and deserves a break. She would also like to spend time with her NT child. Dad should step in and take responsibility for the NLD child, and Mom should help the NT child with his homework. There are several benefits to this approach:

- Mom gets a much-needed break;
- by spending time with the NLD child, Dad becomes more aware of her needs and how best to handle her;
- the sibling gets one-on-one time with Mom, thereby reducing the likelihood of his resentment of the NLD child;
- the marriage is strengthened by Dad's understanding and willingness to assume parental responsibility.

A win for everyone. Of course this assumes that Dad is not resentful himself, immediately getting into a huge argument with the NLD child, and that Mom does not undermine Dad's efforts, thinking that she can do better herself, even if she can.

In a single-parent household, life will be far more challenging. Single parenting is difficult at best. Where the single parent is raising an NLD child, he or she may quickly become as over-whelmed as the child. If there are other children, the job of parenting may become almost impossible. It is critical that the single parent have a strong support system that can provide respite and share the burden of raising a special needs child.

RESPECT FOR ALL FAMILY MEMBERS

It is easy to become immersed in the needs of the impaired child. However, every member of the family must be respected, even if a disproportionate amount of time is required for one child. If there are siblings, make time for them. When your neurologically typical child wants to go shopping at the mall, leave the NLD child with another family member or trusted sitter. You know that the NLD child would probably become overwhelmed on the excursion, and her sibling shouldn't have to suffer the consequences. This will only cause resentment, and more unnecessary stress within the family.

Mom and Dad should also make time for each other. Find time to be alone and talk about something other than the children. Go for a walk or drive together, just to relax. It is important to keep your relationship strong. Having a special date with your partner is good for all relationships, but even more beneficial for the parents of an impaired child who spend so much time meeting her special needs. You were together before the children came along, and hopefully will still be together when they are gone. It is difficult to hold any relationship together today, but even more challenging when there is a special child. You'll have to work at it.

All parents, whether married or single, need to take time for themselves. It is imperative that you incorporate into your schedule occasions where you can be alone in order to recharge your batteries. That might be an hour or so spent with a good book every day, an afternoon on the weekend to escape and enjoy a particular interest, or a long weekend away every few months. Whatever your preference, find the time, and consider it a priority. Although most parents understand that they should find time for themselves, few actually consider it a priority. For single parents, this personal time is absolutely critical, since parenting is even more exhausting when there is no partner to share the burden. When raising a special needs child, it is critical that you maintain your health, perspective, and attitude. If you become worn down by parental responsibilities, you won't have the energy to sustain intervention and caregiving efforts, or to handle crises when they occur – and they will occur. A physically or emotionally depleted parent is far less able to meet the needs of their child(ren), especially if that child has NLD. For single parents who do not have a support system that will allow for parenting breaks, there may be help available through your local social services agency. Be kind to yourself. Seeing to your own needs is one of the best things that you can do for your family.

EXTERNAL PRESSURES

There may also be external pressures on you and your family. Unfortunately, your efforts to do what is right for your NLD child may not be understood by friends and other family members. In fact, they may not recognize that there is a disability at all. You may be accused by many of simply being over-protective, and told by others to 'just leave the child alone – she'll be fine.' No matter how much you try to educate those around you, there will always be some who refuse to accept the disability. It is to be hoped that these won't be the people who matter most to you.

As you are assaulted by those near and dear to you with criticisms of your parenting skills, it will be difficult not to buckle to the temptation of agreeing with them. After all, you don't want your child to have a neurological disability, so maybe they are right. Yes, it's tempting, but selfish. Denial won't help your child, and in the long run, it won't help you either. You would just end up chastising yourself for not being the parent you should be for this special child.

STRESS WITHIN THE FAMILY

In addition to meeting the various needs of the NLD child, there is likely to be considerable stress within the immediate family. Unfortunately, that is to be expected no matter how well you are handling the situation. At times, everything will be fine, possibly for long intervals, and then a crisis will catch you unprepared. It is helpful for the family to have an available support system – either a psychologist, a pastor or rabbi, or another trusted individual who is able to assist the family in handling the ongoing challenges of raising an NLD child. A trusted counselor who knows all of the family members can be quite effective in seeing a situation objectively, and provide advice or options which can work for everyone in order to solve a particular problem.

Naturally, it is prudent to seek help before a crisis occurs, to have someone in place for those times when you, or some other family member, are at the end of your rope. However, if you do find yourself in a crisis, without a support system, your closest children's hospital should have recommendations of psychologists who specialize in children with a developmental disability. Don't hesitate to get help when you need it, whether it is a crisis, or the accumulated stress which is taking a toll on you and your family.

PRIORITIZE THE CHILD'S NEEDS

Once your child has been diagnosed, it is tempting to try and 'fix' as much as possible, as quickly as possible. A program that is too encompassing is difficult to manage, and will simply overwhelm you and the child. Remember that she needs structure and pre-dictability. If she is bounced from one specialist to another, or introduced to too many things to learn at once, she may shut down, and gain no benefit from any of them. Instead, it might be more appropriate to identify the top three issues you want to work on over the course of a year, and direct your efforts to those areas.

Clearly, raising an NLD child is far more challenging and time consuming than you might have anticipated. Unfortunately, we do not have the luxury of 'ordering' a perfect infant. Although your child has a disability, it could be worse. Think of the parents whose child has a life-threatening disease, and realize that the 'luck of the draw' could have been much, much worse. So, play the cards you were dealt, not the ones you want. Cherish the uniqueness of this child – be her tutor as well as her parent, and enjoy her many talents and special charm. Protect her from the very real dangers she will face, but foster a 'can do' attitude, and an expectation that she can succeed – because she can!

SUMMARY

The parent of an NLD child will play the pivotal role in the child's development and intervention program. Beware of the parent traps:

- ○ denial of, or minimizing the child's disability;
- ○ doing for the child what they can do for themselves (learned helplessness);

The parent will need to coordinate, or directly provide, the required support for the child, and act as her:

- ○ *facilitator* – translating for the child, especially the 65 per cent of communication which is nonverbal;
- ○ *social coach* – helping the child to understand unwritten social and cultural rules;
- ○ *advocate* – ensuring that the educational needs of the child are met.

It takes two parents, or a single parent with a very strong support system, to raise an NLD child. Consider the needs of each family member, and carve out personal time from your busy schedule to recharge your batteries.

Unfortunately, many friends and family members will criticize your parenting skills, and there will be significant stress within the family. Don't hesitate to get professional help.

Prioritize the needs of the NLD child in order to increase the likelihood of success.

Chapter 4

Self-help Skills

Basic self-help skills, such as personal hygiene and dressing, are things we introduce our children to at a very early age. Most children learn the concept of clean hands and face, daily baths, washed and combed hair, and so on, quite easily, with little direct instruction. But NLD children won't learn these skills on their own, or not to the extent that we would like. Since it is unlikely that your child was diagnosed before age five, and probably not until they were at least eight years old, you did not have a full appreciation of her difficulties when basic self-help skills were being introduced. You now know that she must be specifically taught what to do, when to do it, and how to do it. Let's consider how we might approach teaching hygiene and dressing in a way that is sensitive to this child's needs and learning style.

HYGIENE

Personal hygiene is important for a number of reasons, the most obvious being health. However, equally important for the NLD child are the implications of poor hygiene on their social relationships. Due to the child's impaired social skills, she will probably have difficulty making and keeping friends, especially as she enters adolescence, when issues of personal hygiene become quite pronounced. Our children will be far more appealing to their peers if they have good hygiene. Although it doesn't become a significant social issue until the upper elementary grades or middle school, the concept of cleanliness must be introduced as young as possible. If good hygiene habits are not ingrained by adolescence, it will be very difficult to address them as a priority at that time, along with all of the other issues she will then be facing.

Another point in favor of good hygiene habits is the impression that they make on adults. Although appearance shouldn't matter, it clearly does. If you want other caregivers and teachers to take a personal interest in your child, present them with one who looks loved and well cared for. A child who is clean, with combed hair, and neatly dressed, is naturally more appealing than one who is dirty, poorly dressed, with unkempt hair. Once hygiene tasks are included as part of the child's daily routine, they will become ingrained simply because they are part of the routine. Of course it isn't actually as easy as it sounds. Let's consider how we might address the NLD child's hygiene issues.

Bathing

Now that we've said that the child should be squeaky clean, we're faced with the challenge of how to get her to accept a bath, have her hair washed, combed, dried, and so on. Some NLD children do not take to a bath like a duck to water. She may actually be terrified of a bath. If this is the case, when she is quite young, it might be wise to get in the tub with her. After all, you wanted a bath anyway, right?

There may be touch and odor sensitivities which cause the child to resist being soaped up and scrubbed – she doesn't like the feel of the washcloth, or the smell of the soap. As an alternative, why not pour some dishwashing liquid into the water, and let her soak in a nice 'bubble' bath. A good choice would be Ivory Liquid (or something similar) which is gentle on her skin, and without a strong scent. The objective is a clean child but maybe you'll get a bonus with a 'bubble' bath – if she isn't in such a hurry to get out, just maybe you'll get a clean, relaxed child.

If it's a hot summer day, and you have access to a swimming pool, let her take a dip before bed instead of having a traditional bath. Or she can run around in a sprinkler, or play with a hose, as long as she gets good and wet and clean. Of course, this assumes that she can handle a change to her routine. The idea is that there are creative solutions to your child's fears and sensitivities. Do whatever works, and make it fun.

Hair – Washing

Now it's on to washing her hair. Simply wetting her hair may bring shrieks of terror, and you haven't even soaped it yet. A word of caution – dumping water over this kid's head is definitely not smart, especially if it comes as a surprise. If you do, you may be hard pressed to ever get her into a tub again. She needs a gentle approach.

Start by explaining to her what you're going to do. Tell her that you're going to be very gentle, and that she can put a washcloth over her eyes so no water gets in them. Show her where the water will come from – whether from a spray or pitcher. (Since many of these children have scalp sensitivities, a pitcher may bother her less than the feel of a spray.) Once in the tub, have her tip her head back, and gently cascade the water through her hair to wet it thoroughly. When it comes to shampooing, try to involve her in the process, and let her play with the suds – take the fear out of the activity. Obviously, you'll want to use baby shampoo or some other form of tearless product. When it's time to rinse, again no surprises – tell her when you're going to do it, let her use the washcloth again to cover her eyes, tip her head back, and again cascade the water through her hair until it rinses clean.

Some children may prefer, or respond better to, having their hair washed in the sink. Have the child lie on her back on a counter so that her head can rest on, or over, the edge of the sink. You can place a folded towel under her neck, and give her a washcloth to cover her eyes. This method may also be physically easier for the parent, who won't need to bend over a tub, while trying to be patient and supportive. Of course this approach won't last too long, unless you have a very long counter. However, for the child who is truly terrified of having her hair washed, it's an option worth considering.

More hair – Combing and drying

Okay, now that we've had such a good time in the bath and having our hair washed, let's move on to some more fun – time to comb her hair. Give yourself (and your child) every advantage – use some spray-in detangler or conditioner. If combing bothers her scalp, you might try a brush with a flexible base and rubber bristles that have 'give' and will move through the hair more easily. If she would rather comb or brush her hair by herself then, by all means, let her do so. You can always touch it up at the end if necessary.

In addition to some NLD children's scalp sensitivity, they may also dislike or be afraid of loud noises. Don't add insult to injury by drying her hair with a hair dryer. For the child with auditory sensitivity, this exercise would be a nightmare – let her hair dry naturally.

If you have a daughter who hates to have her hair messed with, forget the long tresses. Keep it short and easy to care for. Pigtails, braids, ponytails, barrettes – all that scalp pressure may be pure torture for her. For some reason, it always seems to be the Dads who want their daughters to have long hair. If this is the case in your home, then have Dad handle hair washing, combing, and drying, as well as pigtails, braids, or barrettes.

Showers

When it appears that your child is ready to graduate from bath to shower, initially, you might want to get in with them. Since we are talking about an older child, maybe six or seven, it might be wise if you wore a bathing suit, especially if the child is of the opposite sex. This is a big step for these kids, and can be frightening. It is a new task, so they need to be taught all of the new things, and explained how the old ones apply.

Show her that the angle of the showerhead can be changed, and find the position that she likes best. If she doesn't like the water pounding on her all the time, angle it so that she can step under the water, and then out when she chooses to. Continue with the tearless shampoo, if need be, and do so for as long as necessary. After the first few showers, she will probably go in alone, as long as you stay in the bathroom. She may be insecure with the feeling of isolation created by a shower curtain that she can't see through, even if you are in the bathroom with her. If you find this to be the case, a glass shower door, or clear shower curtain might reassure the child. Depending on her age and ability, you might still want to lather her hair, and 'check behind her ears.' Only you can determine how long this should continue. After a few days or weeks, depending on the child, you will probably be able to leave the bathroom, but continue to check on her while she is showering.

Cleaning teeth

Start brushing your child's teeth when she is very young, and make sure that you incorporate it into her overall routine. Try different brands and flavors of toothpaste until you find one that your child likes, especially if she has a strong negative reaction to a particular smell, taste, or texture. Buy a toothbrush with a small head, and be sure and use one with soft bristles. These children tend to press hard when doing something with their hands, and you don't want her damaging her gums. If your child has difficulty handling a toothbrush properly in order to clean all surfaces, try a fun-looking electric toothbrush and see if that helps. As she gets older, and the dentist recommends floss, your child may find floss quite awkward to manipulate. Check with the dentist to see if a water pick would be acceptable. If so, you might want to try that in lieu of the dental floss, carefully explaining how it is to be used.

An automatic routine

In time these habits become ingrained, if only because they are part of the child's daily routine. The routine will become 'automatic' more readily if all tasks are performed every day, rather than baths and/or washing hair only every other day. For these children, routines don't mean different things on different days. Although you may dread the prospect of going through the bath/shower/ hair washing routine on a daily basis, there will come a day when it all pays dividends. You will tell your child it's time to take a shower, which she then does all by herself, without a fuss, and comes out clean! And, she combs her own hair with a straight parting, puts her pajamas on, and puts herself to bed.

You may be thinking that the above discussion about the difficulties of bathing, washing hair, taking showers, and so forth, applies to all children, and you may be right. However, with the NLD child the problems are more extreme and last longer.

Deodorant

Be sure and introduce the child to the purpose and use of deodorant as soon as it becomes apparent that she needs it. Many of these children have a heightened sense of smell. The first indication that the time is right for introducing the concept of body odor and deodorant may be when she complains that so-and-so smells bad. You can then explain that as we get older, even if we take baths, we can have body odor. For that reason, there is deodorant that we can apply under our arms every day so that we don't smell. This may be the best time to have your child begin wearing deodorant. However, take her shopping with you. Remember that she may have negative reactions to certain odors. Take the caps off of the different brands of deodorant in the store, and let her smell several until she finds one that she likes.

Menstrual cycle

Prepare your daughter for the onset of her menstrual cycle. This will almost certainly be an alarming event for your NLD child, regardless of how well prepared she is. She needs to know exactly what to do when there is any indication that she may have started to menstruate. Once her cycle has begun, use a calendar to show her when the next period is likely to begin. Monitor this carefully, and encourage the use of a sanitary napkin a few days prior to the expected monthly onset.

Involve the school nurse in this process. She can be an excellent resource, and will gladly provide reassurance and assistance to your child. Incorporate visits to the nurse's office into your child's daily school routine. Have her change her sanitary napkin there, rather than in the girls' rest room. As she assimilates this monthly event into her normal routine, she can be weaned off the dependence on the nurse. However, understand that this may take several years.

Shaving

During adolescence, your child will be faced with the need to shave. Buy her an electric razor, teach her how to use it, and then remind her when it is apparent that she needs to shave. For boys, this may be daily, or every few days, depending on how rapidly their facial hair grows. For girls, this may be something that is scheduled for once a week.

Do not allow these children to use a straight-edge razor. Their coordination difficulties could cause them serious injury if allowed to use a manual razor.

Do not shave for them once you have taught them how to do it. Supervise the activity once you have taught her how to use the razor, and until you are sure that she is competent, and then a simple reminder is sufficient. Remember that you are trying to encourage independence, and there is little risk of injury from an electric razor.

Trimming nails

Neat and clean finger- and toenails require that they be clipped. Naturally, you will do this task for your child when she is young. However, if you are still performing this task once the child has started to use deodorant, it is time to teach her how to do it for herself. Sit her beside you and verbally explain everything you are doing. Point out that you press the skin away from the nail before cutting it so that you won't cut the skin. Next time it is time to clip her nails, do all but one, again verbally explaining everything you do, and have her clip one nail on her own. Gradually move the task from you doing the majority of the work to your child doing the majority of the clipping, until she is doing the task on her own. Supervise the activity the next few times, and then leave the responsibility up to the child, other than giving a reminder when necessary.

DRESSING

Getting dressed seems such a simple task – well, maybe for us. This is another one of those life skills that we learn almost by instinct, but in reality we learn it through observation. However, observation isn't the learning style of NLD youngsters. As in all other areas, we have to teach them verbally how to dress in a step-by-step fashion. Let's look at how confusing the task is from the child's perspective.

First, she doesn't know in what order to put on each garment. But even if she does, the task is still quite puzzling. She takes her panties, looks at them, then while standing, she tries to put one foot, and then the other through the leg holes, promptly losing her balance. Since she has limited observational skills, and even weaker nonverbal problem solving skills, she doesn't realize that the task would be easier if she were sitting down. Next she tries putting on her T-shirt, and hasn't a clue as to what to do first. Out of frustration, she tosses the T-shirt on the floor and has a temper tantrum, screaming 'I can't do this!' and the day has barely begun.

Putting on clothing

Since these kids need to have things explained to them verbally, it would be more helpful to approach teaching the child how to dress in a very direct, scripted manner.

First, lay out the clothes on her bed in the order in which they are to be put on. On the top of the pile would be her panties, followed by a T-shirt, then her pants, shirt, and socks. We'll get to the shoes later.

Tell her to sit on the edge of the bed: 'Okay sweetheart, it's time to get dressed. First, we'll put your panties on. So, I need you to sit on the edge of the bed so that when you put your feet through the leg openings of your panties, you won't lose your balance and fall down.' You show her that the waist hole is larger than the two leg holes, how to tell which is the front versus the back, and position the panties in front of her, holding the waist open. 'Okay, put one leg through the first small hole, and then the other leg through the other small hole. Now, before I can pull your panties all the way up, you'll have to slide off of the bed so that I can get them over your bottom.' You talk her through every step of the way, in simple but very specific language.

Next is the T-shirt, which you might consider eliminating entirely unless you live in a very cold climate. It's one more step to learn in the dressing routine. However, if the T-shirt is necessary, putting it on would go something like this: 'The next thing that we do is put on your T-shirt. This has four holes in it. Your head and arms will go through the biggest one, and then through a smaller hole. The hole on top is for your head, and the holes on each side are for your arms.' Show her the holes as you are describing them. 'Okay, now the T-shirt goes over your head, and your head goes through the smaller hole at the top. Now one arm goes through one side hole, and the other arm goes through the other side hole.'

We've only done panties and T-shirt, and it probably sounds very tedious. However, breaking all of the tasks down into their smallest component steps, verbally scripting as you go, is quite necessary if the NLD child is to learn. You need to go through the same process with pants and shirt, verbally repeating every step again as you put on each garment.

Socks are a bit tricky. The most effective way to teach the child how to put them on is by being behind the child's leg (they could sit on your lap, or next to you with their leg on your lap), again verbalizing what you are doing as you do it.

Shoes and shoelaces

Ugh, shoes! Actually shoes aren't the problem, it's the shoelaces that are a nightmare. When your child is young, it might be best simply to avoid shoes which require lacing. Shoes with Velcro closures are wonderful. Fortunately, shoes with Velcro closures are quite easy to find, even for the older child. Another option to laced shoes is sandals, which are obviously terrific in the summer. In many areas, sandals with heavy socks are worn year round, and this might be a good option for the NLD child. It's difficult enough to teach her all of the other tasks involved in dressing, without adding the complication of tying shoelaces. However, at some point, you'll be faced with having to teach this skill as well. For most of these kids, it is simple repetition – again, verbalizing every step you go through, from putting the shoe on, to making sure her heel is all the way down in the shoe, to tightening and tying the laces.

Buttons and zippers

Buttons and zippers are incredibly difficult for NLD youngsters to manage. Wherever possible, try to avoid them – buy elastic-waist pants, a jacket with Velcro closures, anything to avoid adding one more complication to her already difficult task of getting dressed. It's also important to keep in mind that you're trying to raise a confident, independent child. The easier that you can make it for her to accomplish any form of independence, the better you are doing your job as a parent.

It is more effective for the child to learn how to get a button through a buttonhole, or zip a zipper when the garment is not on her. Provide her with materials that she can practice on, and teach these skills before you expect her to do them while wearing the garment. Larger buttons are easier, so select garments with larger buttons whenever you can. Also, attaching pulls to zippers will help her with this task.

Clearly, the easiest time to start teaching your child how to dress herself is during the warm summer months when she is wearing fewer clothes. However, long before then, start the scripting process as you dress her yourself. Don't skip any step, no matter how small it might seem. If you skip a step thinking that it is too minor, when she tries to do it by herself, she will get stuck at that exact place and not be able to go further.

Don't be surprised if your child is upwards of seven or eight years old before she is able to dress herself capably. Even then, you may still be laying her clothes out for her. And always, always, allow plenty of time for her to get dressed. If she is rushed, she will likely become confused and be unable to perform the task on her own.

Buy peer-friendly clothes

When selecting your child's clothes, be sensitive to what her peer group is wearing. Remember that you want your child to be accepted, not be more socially isolated because of her wardrobe. Also, sometime between third and fifth grade, involve her in the process of observing what the other kids wear. Do they wear a particular type of shoe? Are bell-bottom jeans the fad, or is it baggy jeans?

Naturally, you want to maintain a certain level of control to make sure that your child is dressed appropriately for your own personal standards. However, the idea is for her to become more aware – for her to understand what is peer acceptable versus 'geeky.' If she doesn't 'get it' by observing her peer group, then use examples that she can relate to and understand more readily. As insensitive as it may sound, you may need to point out a child that is shunned at school because of their appearance. Explain the differences that set that child apart. An example that may help her to understand is the character Steven Erkel from the television show *Family Matters*. If you haven't seen him, he was the 'geeky' kid with his suspendered pants pulled up high, so that the waist was clearly well above where it should have been. Explain to her that, like Steven Erkel, there are kids at school who are ostracized because of their appearance. Teach your child how to avoid presenting an 'odd' appearance.

As your child starts middle school, there may be an administration policy that all children should change their clothes for gym. Since these children are not particularly adept at changing their clothes, and certainly not quickly, this requirement should be waived. Make sure that on gym days, the child is wearing clothes appropriate for physical activity, including sneakers. If it is possible for the school to schedule your child's gym class for the last period of the day, that would be ideal. Then she won't have to spend the day in sweaty, smelly, and possibly dirty clothes!

THE OCCUPATIONAL THERAPIST

Being neat, clean and dressed in socially accepted clothing will give your child a social advantage, something that she needs very much. These children can certainly be taught good personal hygiene, and by adolescence should be well on their way to independence in this area.

If your child seems to have inordinate problems in the area of self-help skills, you may want to involve an occupational therapist. An occupational therapist is trained to help individuals improve their ability to perform tasks for independent living if functions are impaired. Most schools have occupational therapists on staff. You may request an occupational therapy evaluation, and if the determination is that your child needs this type of intervention, the school will incorporate it into their educational plan.

Although your child may not require a full occupational therapy intervention plan, there may be certain tasks that she is unable to perform. For instance, if your child is unable to tie her shoelaces by the time she is in first or second grade, it would be helpful to enlist the aid of the school's occupational therapist to teach her how to do so. This may only require a few sessions, and you may not need an individualized education plan in order to obtain this limited assistance.

SUMMARY
Hygiene

- Establish a hygiene routine when the child is young so that it is ingrained by the time she reaches adolescence.

- Be sensitive to the NLD child's fears, such as bathing, showering, hair washing, or being unable to see you while she is in the shower or tub.

- Be considerate of the child's other sensitivities, such as the smell of soap, being scrubbed with a washcloth, or having her hair combed and dried.

- Teach her the whys and hows of using deodorant, as well as how to clip her own nails.

- For shaving, teach the child how to use an electric razor, and never allow the use of a straight-edge razor.

- Be sure that your daughter is very well prepared for the onset of her menstrual cycle, and enlist the aid of the school nurse.

Dressing

- ° Lay the child's clothes out in the order in which she will put them on.

- ° Teach her how to dress in a verbally scripted, step-by-step fashion. Start the scripting process long before you actually begin to teach her how to dress herself.

- ° Shoes with Velcro closures or sandals are much easier for the child than those with shoelaces.

- ° Buttons and zippers are very difficult. Buy pants with an elastic waist and jackets with Velcro closures.

- ° Start the actual teaching to dress process in the warm summer months when the child is wearing fewer garments.

- ° Buy peer-friendly clothes, and teach the child how to present a socially acceptable rather than odd appearance.

- ° Enlist the aid of an occupational therapist if the child's self-help skills are severely impaired.

Chapter 5

Fine Motor Skills

Deficits in fine motor skills may be one of the first things that you notice in your NLD child. At an early age, the difficulties in fine motor skills are generally fairly obvious. You may notice that she has difficulty holding her toothbrush, putting a button through a buttonhole, eating with a spoon or coloring with a crayon. There are many fun activities that you can do at home which will improve your child's finger dexterity, while at the same time increasing her confidence. The first half of this chapter will cover arts, crafts and games to improve fine motor skills, and the second half of the chapter will address eating and writing instruments.

ARTS, CRAFTS, AND GAMES

Although you want to encourage arts and crafts to foster creativity and improve your child's fine motor skills, be sure to select mediums and levels of difficulty that are appropriate for your child's ability, not her chronological age. Keep in mind that you may be faced with tactile defensiveness issues – things that your child just can't tolerate the feel of. For instance, most children love using finger paints – getting it all over their hands, feeling it squish through their fingers and then smearing it all over a piece of paper. However, your child may absolutely hate the feel of paint on her fingers. If your child has tactile issues, introduce her to various mediums, but if she has a negative reaction to one, don't force it on her.

The idea of using arts, crafts, and games to improve fine motor skills and finger dexterity is so that the child enjoys what she is doing without feeling like it is work. She will make the best progress if she is simply having a good time. Don't force her into an activity because it seems like fun to you. It needs to be fun for her, and she has her own unique sense of what is enjoyable.

In order to improve fine motor skills, you must work on the major muscle groups as well. Therefore, in order to increase her finger dexterity, you'll also be working to strengthen her shoulder and arm muscles, which in turn benefits her wrist and hand movement. To have good coordinated movement, everything must be working together, so that no part of the body is forced to compensate for another.

The following are some ideas of activities that your child may enjoy while developing improved fine motor function.

- Put large pieces of paper up on the wall of the basement, garage, or wherever you have the space and don't mind the mess. Give your child a large art paintbrush, preferably with a fat handle. Put paint in spill-proof cups, and turn her loose! Encourage her to use her entire arm in the activity, making big sweeping strokes.

- For young children, buy paint-with-water books. These are books that change color when you 'paint' an area with water. This allows the child to 'paint' a picture that looks nice when it's done, while avoiding the frustration of being unable to stay within the lines. The outlines of the objects are clearly marked on the page, so that you can encourage her to practice staying within the lines, but she can't possibly make a mistake. A wonderful confidence booster for the younger child who gets frustrated with her attempts at painting.

○ For children who have mastered staying between the lines, paint-by-number pictures are wonderful. The child doesn't have to try and draw the outline, or figure out what color to use where in order to paint a more sophisticated picture. The outlines are already drawn for her, and the directions explain which number represents which color. There are a variety of levels of difficulty so that children of various ages can enjoy this activity. The finished product might be quite impressive.

○ Stencils allow another way for a child to make pictures. You can purchase hard plastic sheets with all kinds of characters and shapes on them which the child can trace and then fill in. You might sketch a background for her of a room, or the yard, and she can then add the people, animals, flowers, sun, and so forth to complete the picture.

○ Encourage any kind of craft projects. The older kids may enjoy the symmetry of making key chains and so forth out of gimp (flat vinyl craft lacing). Many youngsters learn how to do this during summer camp, but you can buy kits at a developmental toy store, and teach the child yourself.

○ Experiment with various types of clay – there are a variety of textures, and some will be enjoyed more than others. You can buy plain clay that she can paint, or colored clay that needs no painting. For older children, the colored modeling product FIMO is wonderful. She can make figurines, beads, or any number of small items. When she has finished her project, it is baked in the oven to harden. The variety of colors is incredible, and the result of the child's work looks quite good once it is baked.

○ Mr. and Mrs. Potato Head are terrific for these children, but buy the plastic potato (rather than using a real one) because they have pre-drilled holes where the various parts go (eyes, ears, nose and so forth). This is much easier for the NLD child than forcing the parts into a real potato.

Not only does this activity improve her finger dexterity, putting the different hats, eyes, ears, etc. in the head, but you can practice different facial images – make them look silly, happy, or whatever. This is a fun activity where you are reinforcing more than one skill.

○ Colorforms (a very thin vinyl material) are a wonderful invention. You can buy them in shapes of various colors for her to make designs with, or you can buy a colorforms kit of her favorite television or movie characters. Although colorforms generally adhere to a specific type of paper, they work wonderfully on windows and glass doors as well. You may find your child sitting in front of a large window or glass door for hours, moving the characters around, or elaborating on her masterpiece.

○ A great new invention is similar to colorforms, but used on the walls of a child's room to decorate it. There are kits you can buy at a paint or wallpaper store that have borders that can be placed at any height in a room simply by sticking it to the wall. The beauty is that the border can be easily peeled off and repositioned. The kits come with dozens of smaller pieces to place on or around the border. An example would be a blue border shaped like waves, with all types of fish, shells, treasure chests, sea gulls and clouds. Your child can truly help decorate her bedroom in the motif of her choice. This should be a parent and child activity, so that you can assist her with the more awkward placements. Not only does it improve her finger dexterity, but you can point out what might go where based on the characteristics of the object. This will encourage her to look at both the big picture and where the pieces fit into the whole. As the child gets older, and you want to change the appearance of her room, you simply peel off the border and smaller items. You can then shop for another kit which is appropriate for the child's age, and redecorate the room together again. A wonderfully creative exercise.

○ Jigsaw puzzles are terrific for teaching the relationship of parts to whole as well as exercising fine motor dexterity. For very young children, simple shapes are best. Some come with little handles on the pieces which may be easier for the child to manipulate. The best puzzles are the rubberized ones which are more forgiving if the child can't get the pieces to fit exactly. These puzzles are sold at varying levels of difficulty, from very basic formats to others that are quite complex. Therefore, they are appropriate for a wide range of ages. Older children can make a rather sophisticated puzzle-picture more easily than they might with other mediums, and they are developing basic problem solving skills by determining which piece goes where.

○ Another great activity that is very inexpensive is to allow the child to use sidewalk chalk on your walkway or driveway. This type of chalk is very fat, comes in great colors, doesn't break as easily as regular chalk for those who press very heavy when they draw, and it lasts forever. She can have a terrific time making huge designs and pictures, and the beauty is that with the first rain, it's all washed away! Warn her of this eventuality, however, because she may be devastated to find her wonderful project has disappeared with the first rain shower.

○ Crayons may actually be the least favored medium for the young NLD child. They break quite easily, are thin and difficult to hold, and mistakes can't be corrected. If this is the case for your child, you might consider colored pencils that can be erased. If she likes crayons but has difficulty holding them in a traditional grasp, there are now crayons available that are shaped like a big fat teardrop. These are 'palmed' in the child's hand, may be easier for her to use, and are incredibly sturdy.

○ Building models are a wonderful exercise for these children. The kits are numbered or coded on the packaging by degree of skill required to assemble them. The less demanding models do not even require the use of glue or paint. The rather large pre-colored parts simply snap together. As the degree of difficulty increases, the use of glue and painting is added, the parts get smaller and are more numerous, and painting graduates to more demanding levels. You may reduce the child's possible frustration with this activity if you select an item that particularly appeals to her. For instance, if she has a Titanic fetish, then buying a model of the Titanic may well inspire her to tackle what might otherwise seem too difficult for her.

- A wonderful little product is called Wicky Sticks. Wicky Sticks are very thin strips of colored wax. They stick to a piece of paper, but can be readily lifted off. These are a very simple but brilliant invention which can be used in a variety of ways. If the child continues to have difficulty grasping a crayon, paintbrush, or other instrument, the Wicky Sticks can be used creatively. You can cut them in varying lengths and the child can 'draw' her pictures by shaping the sticks and placing them on a piece of paper. A piece of yellow can be shaped into a circle for the sun, with shorter pieces for the rays. She can make stick figures for people and animals, trees, grass, or whatever she wants. However, since she may have difficulty with scissors, you will need to cut the pieces for her. Again, this would be a good parent and child activity so that you can discuss with her what things might be in the picture, improving her visual awareness of what one might expect to see, based on the picture that she is creating. Should there be trees, a house, or barn? Is it daytime or nighttime? Then we should include either a sun or a moon and stars. Help her put together the whole image.

- If the child has difficulty learning physically to write the alphabet or her name, you can use Wicky Sticks for this as well. She may be able to shape the pieces of sticks onto paper to form a letter, or her name, more readily than trying to use a traditional writing instrument. Fixing mistakes is as simple as lifting the section of sticks off the paper and repositioning it.

○ Another suggestion for teaching these children to write is to use a sand tray. This can be made quite easily by pouring sanitized sand onto a baking tray which has low sides. The child can practice tracing letters or her name in the sand. If she makes a mistake, she can easily 'erase' it, and start again.

○ Alphabet magnets are a really nice tool to use for spelling. Teachers suggest that you use both upper and lower case letters when you introduce them. Apparently that is the way that students are taught when they get to school, so you should be consistent. In any event, you can use a baking tray for this also. She can 'write' words by attaching the letter magnets to the tray, and although the magnets stay put, corrections are as easy as lifting the magnet off of the tray. You might encourage the child to 'write' on your refrigerator too, which she will probably think is great fun. Just watch those magnets around electronics, or you might find that your television no longer works.

○ There is a product called Lite Brites which is terrific for NLD kids. It's similar to a shadow box, in that it is a box with an electrical light inside. The front has slots for inserting black sheets of paper that have codes on them. The codes correlate to colors of little lights that you plug into preformed holes in the blackpaper. Once the child has put all of the little lights in all of the appropriate holes, the lights form a picture. This is great for finger dexterity, and the finished product is very exciting for the child. The manufacturer sells separate extra packets of pictures, so there are many different sheets that the child can do. There is a rather broad age range for this product, as some of the pictures are very simple, and others quite difficult. The sheets are reusable so that the child can create the same picture several times. This is great for finger dexterity as well as for hand–eye coordination.

○ Stringing beads is a simple, fun activity. For the young child, or for the older child who continues to struggle with finger dexterity, use a very large blunt needle, and a heavy-gauge string or other medium and large beads. As the child improves, use a smaller needle, thinner string, and smaller beads. This is another activity that improves finger dexterity as well as hand–eye coordination.

○ As the child's finger dexterity improves, she may enjoy playing a game called Jenga. This game consists of a tall tower of stacked, long, slender blocks. The object is to slide out a block from somewhere in the tower, and place the block carefully on top of the tower without it toppling over. This is great fun for both older children and adults. You'll almost certainly enjoy it as much as your child does. It's a great hand–eye coordination activity that also teaches weight displacement. Some NLD children get quite proficient at this game!

Since you are trying to teach and develop fine motor skills, it's not a bad idea to stretch the limit of the child's ability just a bit. However, do not set her up to fail. You may not have noticed, but none of these activities (with the possible exception of the Wicky Sticks) requires the use of scissors. That is intentional because, for these children, scissors are likely to be quite difficult to master, if they ever can. Identify the areas of deficit that may be too severe to improve, or should wait until she is older. Then, select activities that can strengthen her other skill deficits.

EATING AND WRITING INSTRUMENTS

Holding an eating utensil may come quite late for your child. The task of holding a utensil properly, getting food onto it, and directing it to the mouth, all while keeping the food from falling off, can be incredibly difficult for the child. She may prefer to use her fingers for far longer than you think is cute. However, think about what you would do if you were hungry and there were no eating utensils available – you'd eat with your hands too. Yes, there are utensils available to them, but what a chore. The following are some thoughts that you might find helpful in improving your child's use of utensils.

- ° Start with trying to accomplish your primary objective, which is to wean your child off of using her fingers. Avoid starting before she is able. If she can't hold a crayon or paintbrush, how can you expect her to hold an eating utensil, and get food on it, and then in her mouth? Very simply, you can't. So watch and wait, and when you feel that she does have the ability to start, begin by using a spoon or fork depending on what is easier for her. A spoon may be easier for peas, while a fork may be easier to spear beans.

- ° Also, consider using a soup spoon rather than a teaspoon when the child eats cereal, or she is apt to have only one flake and no milk in the spoon by the time it reaches her mouth.

- ° It is also an excellent idea to use utensils with fat handles which are easier to grasp.

- ° Using plates may be adding difficulty to the task. Food slips off the edge, oh-so-easily. Consider using a large shallow bowl so that she can push the food against the side of the bowl to get it on the utensil.

- Although glasses or cups may not be considered a utensil, it seems to fit here. Because these kids are awkward, it is a good idea to use short, bottom-heavy glasses or cups. Tall, lightweight cups or glasses are easily knocked over, angering a sibling, frustrating a parent, and causing more stress for the NLD child.

Give her every advantage when she is tackling mealtime skills – she needs your creativity to help her learn. Don't decide that you want to start introducing eating utensils when the child is starving. You'll be in for a stormy dinner, and the child will learn nothing, except to dread mealtime. And yes, you will probably be cutting her meat for a long time. Take it one step at a time. If taught with patience, she will learn how to use eating utensils effectively.

Writing instruments, as with crayons and eating utensils, will probably be difficult for the child to master. In addition to having difficulty holding it properly, she may tend to press too hard while forming her letters, resulting in a broken pencil or torn paper (you may hear this referred to as dysgraphia). Imagine being on the last line of a homework assignment, only to have the paper rip in half, destroying your long hard work. Talk about frustration! There are many things that might help your child. The following are some ideas to consider, which may trigger ideas of your own:

- When she is first learning to write, she might do best with a very fat pencil with heavy lead. She may find the fat pencil easier to grasp, and the lead will make a heavier line without the need to press down hard.

- Like other children, she will need pre-lined paper, but she may need it longer than her peers.

- Most early elementary teachers have these little gizmos that slip on the child's pencil with indentations where the fingers should rest. They are wonderful at helping children place their fingers in the proper position. If you are unable to find them at an office supply store, check with your child's teacher, or a special education teacher, and they would probably be happy to give you a supply to use at home.

○ For the older child, consider the use of a mechanical pencil. Your first thought may be – won't the lead snap if they press too hard? Yes, and that's part of the point (no pun intended). The idea is to teach your child not to press too hard, or the lead will snap. Use soft lead, otherwise the lead will be constantly breaking. An added bonus with mechanical pencils is that the child won't have to get up to sharpen her pencil every few minutes, thereby breaking her concentration.

○ When shopping for writing instruments, take the child with you. Let her use several to see how they feel in her hand – how easy is one over another to write with? Let her select one or an assortment of instruments to try. Keep trying new ones until she finds one that works best. And if she absolutely loves that screaming pink pencil, buy it. It just might encourage her to try harder.

○ There are great new mechanical pencils that are fat, with cushioning where the fingers are placed – some even have gel. These are far more comfortable than a conventional pencil for the child who holds her pencil in a death grip.

○ If the child must graduate to ink, it would be a good idea to buy pens with erasable ink. However, it would be better still if these children were allowed to use pencils forever. Because their handwriting tends to be poor, especially in the elementary grades, their assignments generally appear sloppy. Requiring that assignments be done in ink will probably mean crossed out words or smudged ink, certainly not enhancing the appearance of their work. Pencils allow the child to self-correct, thereby resulting in a cleaner-looking assignment, increasing her pride in her accomplishment.

The mechanics of writing are difficult and stressful for the NLD child. Provide her with the right tool(s). She will be required to deal with this deficit for many, many years, especially while she is in school. Make the exercise as comfortable as possible for her, for it will probably never be easy.

SUMMARY
Arts, crafts, and games

- Select mediums such as sidewalk chalk which use the shoulder muscles, as well as those of the arm and hand. Developing all muscle groups means that no part of the body has to compensate for another.

- For painting activities, try hanging large pieces of paper on the wall and using a fat paintbrush, using paint-with-water books, paint-by-number kits, and stencils. Colored pencils and teardrop-shaped crayons may be better than regular crayons.

- Colorforms and Wicky Sticks are alternatives to traditional mediums for writing or making pictures.

- Sand trays and magnetic letters are often helpful in teaching the child to write and spell.

- Mr. or Mrs. Potato Head, Lite Brites, clay, and stringing beads are all excellent activities for improving finger dexterity for the younger child, as are simple jigsaw puzzles and models.

- FIMO, Jenga, gimp, and more complex jigsaw puzzles and models are great skill-building activities for the older child.

- Decorate the child's bedroom with stick-on borders and companion pieces.

Eating and writing instruments

○ Eating utensils with fat handles are easier to use.

○ Allow the child to use a spoon or fork – whichever works better – and allow a soup spoon for cereal.

○ Serve the child's food in a large shallow bowl rather than on a flat plate, so food is easier to get onto the utensil and less likely to slip off of the plate.

○ Use bottom-heavy glasses or cups to reduce the likelihood of accidents at the table.

○ When first learning to write, provide the child with a fat pencil which has heavy lead. Use aids on pencils which allow for correct finger positioning.

○ Encourage the use of mechanical pencils to teach correct pressure, preferably with cushioning to reduce finger and hand fatigue.

○ If the child must use pens, buy those with erasable ink.

○ Allow the child to select whatever feels most comfortable.

Chapter 6

Coordination, Athletics, and Team Sports

Looking back at NLD children as babies, probably all parents would agree that they questioned the physical development of their child – not because of pronounced difficulties, but those small nagging issues that just kept popping up. It may have been that the child's early stages of walking appeared more unsteady than might be expected, or that she seemed to take longer to begin alternating feet while climbing the stairs, or a whole host of 'little' uncertainties about whether or not their child was developing normally. They may also have noticed that the child's muscle tone seemed somewhat flaccid. Almost certainly, at an early age, the child was considered awkward and uncoordinated.

As time went by, you probably began to hover ever closer as your child had more falls and scrapes than might be typical of her peers. These are not the children who would be called little mountain goats. Although they may climb, it is with uncertainty, as they try to figure out where to put their feet and hands.

There are several things at play here. These children have spatial difficulties, so they aren't attuned to where they are in relation to other objects or people. They have deficient nonverbal problem solving skills, so merely looking at a physical challenge, such as a large boulder they want to climb, will not provide them with a cue as to what to do next. They don't have the natural coordination of their peers. So let's figure out what might go awry.

THE AWKWARD CHILD

The NLD child sees other youngsters climbing all over a large boulder and having great fun. Wanting to participate and enjoy the activity, she cautiously approaches the boulder. She then begins to try and climb, but does not know to place her feet in natural indentations in the rock, which might make good footholds, because she doesn't 'look and learn' – she can't process information by watching the other children. Her hands do not feel for crevices or natural ledges to hang onto. But with a bit of luck, she manages to get several feet off of the ground, is in a very precarious position, and suddenly freezes. She's stuck, and without a verbal script, she can go no further. You try to tell her to put her feet 'there – on that ledge,' – but you're pointing. She shrieks 'WHERE?' and begins to panic. Unfortunately, a verbal script at this point is useless because, although you are using your voice, you are actually expecting the child to use visual perception and spatial awareness to extricate herself from the situation. Now she starts to slip, scraping knees and fingers, and she is quickly in full-blown panic mode. Can you get to her in time? Or will it mean yet another trip to the hospital emergency room?

At this point, you might be thinking the child would be safer in a plastic bubble for the rest of her life. While a tempting thought, it's obviously not the answer. Instead, you need to teach the child how to tackle a physical task before she attempts this type of activity. It might go something like this.

Your child sees other children climbing on a large boulder. You ask your child if she wants to climb on the boulder too. When she says yes, you approach the boulder with her. Before she starts to climb, you explain what she will have to do. 'This rock is pretty big. It's much bigger than you are! Do you want to climb to the top, and then come back down to me? Or, do you want to climb to the top, and then climb down the other side?' You walk around to the other side of the rock and note that it's too steep; so you tell the child 'I don't think it would be a good idea to try to climb down this side, because it is too steep, and you might easily fall.' So back you both march to the front side of the boulder. You then explain that she will have to place her feet in safe places so that she doesn't lose her footing, and you show her the first natural place, and others as well. Following this, you explain that she will also have to find handholds. Just like she uses the banister when she walks up and down the stairs, she will need something to hold onto so that she doesn't fall while climbing the rock. It might also be helpful to use the stairs analogy to explain the order of alternating her feet, and moving her hands upward as she goes along. So now, it's time for her to start the climb, and off she goes. If this is a young child, it would be wise to climb up behind her so that you can retrieve her more readily in the event that she gets stuck. If she is an older child, you cross your fingers, hold your breath, and pray that she doesn't get stuck or hurt.

It sure does seem like a lot of work just to teach a youngster how to climb a big rock. But think for a moment – if it's a lot of work for you, just think how hard it is for her. It's no wonder she may avoid physical challenges. And even though you may be silently relieved each time she avoids a potentially harmful situation, it's probably not the best thing for her. It would seem better to approach these situations by encouraging her to participate, while you are there to teach her what to do. The more you try and protect her from normal childhood activities such as climbing a rock, the more likely it will be that she is thrust into a situation for which she is unprepared. Friends may encourage her – either innocently, or maliciously – to participate in some type of climbing activity where she could be seriously hurt if she doesn't know what to do. She may never be a mountain goat, but you can teach her some basic skills, and hope that she generalizes them to a new situation if need be.

COORDINATION

As you play with your child, you may find that she has tremendous difficulty throwing and catching a ball, and might actually turn away or duck if a ball is thrown toward her. She probably can't manage to swing a baseball bat and connect with the ball. It is likely that her balance is poor, and she may seem to fall a lot. She may appear to have an awkward gait, and when she runs, it may become more noticeable. Learning to swing on a swing set probably won't come naturally to her as it seems to with other youngsters. If she tries to kick a ball, especially if she is running toward it, she may fall instead, either because she tripped, or lost her balance when she picked her foot up to kick.

NLD children often have difficulty with hopping, skipping, and/or jumping. You won't often find them playing hopscotch or jump rope or jumping from place to place. That is because they find it very difficult to coordinate both sides of their body in a physical activity. These skills are whole-brain tasks and, as you read in Chapter 1, one of their hemispheres (the right) is not working properly. Therefore, the two hemispheres of their brain are not working in concert to allow the body to perform a physical task which requires that both sides of the body work together.

A hallmark of NLD is that these children have tremendous difficulty learning to ride a bicycle, possibly even a tricycle. There is a lot for her to manage – she has to stay balanced on the seat, pedal by alternating pressure on each foot, steer so that she doesn't bump into something, and determine how fast or slowly to go in order to maintain her balance. It takes an incredible amount of practice before most NLD children master riding a two-wheel bicycle. You may wonder if she ever will, and then one day she does; however it is likely to be well after her peers have been riding for some time.

SPORTS
Team sports

Individual physical activities are extremely challenging, and become more difficult when other children are added to the equation. Clearly, the most challenging physical activities for NLD children are team sports. Not only is the child uncoordinated, but she is probably mystified by the rules of play. When you think about it from her perspective, the rules are quite puzzling. Let's use baseball as an example, and discuss the rules when you are at bat.

If you hit the ball and it stays within the first and third base lines, it's okay to run; if it's outside of those two lines, it's considered a foul. If someone on the other team catches it before it hits the ground, you're out, but if they don't, you're safe. You're only supposed to swing at the ball if it is inside or outside the batting zone. There are strikes when you swing and miss, and fouls that are considered strikes. But, since you can't strikeout from fouls, the third foul isn't considered a strike. It's all very confusing.

The child is trying with all of her might to use a skinny stick to hit that little white ball coming at her – and then she does. And then she is confronted with further confusing rules: surprise, surprise you managed to hit the ball, and it stayed between those two lines. Someone tells you to run to first base, so you do. Now the next batter is up – do you run or stay? If it isn't caught, you run, but if it is, you need to stay, or you can be 'thrown out.'

Try scripting all of those rules for the NLD child! All of the 'if this, then that' has the child completely confused and overwhelmed. Add to that all the screaming and shouting, the jeering and cheering, and the child can't think. And then there's the best part – when she's sitting on the bench, waiting for her turn at bat, there's all that awful socializing going on. And this is supposed to be *fun*?

To make matters worse, these children will be mortified if they make a mistake, especially one that brings them ridicule from their teammates. If they are willing, it might be more rewarding for them to act as an umpire or referee. They are more apt to learn the rules if it doesn't require that they do something physical at the same time. Involve the child in some type of activity that makes her feel part of the team without setting her up to fail.

Individual sports

Individual sports are ideal for NLD children. There are many non-competitive, non-team sports at which they can excel. As the child is introduced to any new sport, it is wise to provide her with private lessons if at all possible. Groups of youngsters tend to be noisy, chaotic, and overwhelming for our children. If placed in a group situation, she may give up due to the environmental, rather than the physical, demands. Two organizations are excellent resources to contact in order to locate instructors for NLD children – the Special Olympics, and the Easter Seals society (see Appendix IV for contact details of both organizations). Both groups work with physically challenged children, and know of instructors who would be well suited to the difficulties faced by your child. The following sports are highly recommended for NLD children.

- ° Swimming is ideally suited to NLD youngsters. Although she may not develop classic 'form,' she will likely enjoy the activity in any event. There is no reason that the child can't participate on a swim team at almost any age, assuming that she wants to. The one caution is to make sure that the team is a supportive, non-competitive group, with a good coach who understands the needs of all of the children. The one drawback to swimming is that often there isn't access to an indoor swimming pool during the cold months. If you live in an area where it is too cold to swim outdoors in the winter, and your town does not have an indoor pool, there are other options. One obvious option is a YWCA or YMCA in a surrounding town. If your pediatrician is willing to document the need for access to a swimming pool, there are two additional options. The first is to contact Easter Seals who have wonderful facilities located around the country. With documentation from your child's doctor, you should have no difficulty gaining access to an Easter Seals facility that has an indoor swimming pool. The second option is that many towns without an indoor pool make arrangements with surrounding towns that do have indoor pools for their residents who have special circumstances. Again, your documentation should qualify you for 'special circumstances' pool time with a neighboring town. Also, many colleges allow open pool time for families, or children requiring pool access for therapeutic purposes. A final thought on swimming is that it is not only terrific exercise, but it is also a good idea to teach your child how to swim for safety reasons. Because NLD children are accident prone, she could easily fall into a neighbor's pool, or walk on thin ice which then breaks under her weight, or fall victim to any number of other water hazards. Being able to swim might actually save her life.

○ Ice-skating, roller-skating, and in-line skating are all great individual sports. They are also good non-competitive 'social' sports. Yes, she may well have difficulty with balance, and the demand for precise feet movements, but the training will be excellent. Private instruction is again recommended, and Special Olympics is a good resource for finding a skating instructor. An added benefit to one-on-one instruction with private ice-skating lessons is that when private lessons are scheduled, the only people allowed on the ice are other individuals taking lessons. Therefore, there is far less noise to cope with than during 'open skate' time. The noise level in rinks may be overwhelming for your child, so select carefully when you go, or provide her with earplugs when she is not having lessons. Whether it's ice-skating, roller-skating or in-line skating, don't forget the importance of protective equipment – a good helmet, as well as wrist, elbow, and kneepads.

○ Another recommended individual sport is tennis. Even though your child will have to play against someone, it may not be as competitive as team sports, and certainly doesn't have the huge social component of a team sport. Private instruction is recommended here as well, at least until your child is fairly competent, and then small-group instruction might be very beneficial for the social contact. The major challenge with tennis is that the child will have to cross midline (the invisible line from the top of the head down the body, separating right from left) when she swings the racket. Crossing midline is difficult because it requires that the two sides of the body perform an integrated activity. Although tennis may be challenging, with practice it should improve, but only if the child enjoys what she is doing. An oversized tennis racket (larger surface) and yellow balls (easier to see) will provide additional support as she learns this sport.

○ Golf may be a particularly good choice for NLD children. It is less physically taxing than many other sports, and also tends to be less competitive. Like tennis, the child will probably have difficulty crossing midline, but also like tennis, this should improve with practice. Yellow or other colored balls would help her 'track' where the ball is hit, as well as making it easier to find.

○ A great year-round sport for these kids is archery, and this is probably the least taxing of all of the recommended sports. Correct posture is a key to this sport, and instruction in body awareness and positioning would likely benefit all NLD kids. It is a very controlled activity, not requiring rapid physical responses, and there are indoor as well as outdoor ranges. Many archery facilities sponsor non-competitive teams, allowing the child to 'compete' at her level of ability. Private lessons should be available at any year-round indoor facility. Also, remember that this is a classic sport taught at US summer camps. So, if your child is attending summer camp, encourage her involvement in archery. Although there is little required equipment for archery, an arm guard is an absolute necessity. Make sure that she has a good arm guard so that she does not injure herself when she releases the bowstring.

○ Horseback riding may be a wonderful option for your child, especially if she has a love of animals. Many stables have begun therapeutic programs for challenged youngsters. Instructors trained in animal therapy would have the necessary knowledge to help your child overcome whatever fear she may have, work on balance issues, and develop good riding skills. As with archery, this is a sport where posture is quite important, so that instruction in body awareness and correct posture will be of significant benefit. And don't forget her safety helmet!

○ Learning to paddle a canoe can be great fun for both the child and the entire family. There is the difficulty of crossing midline with this sport, as with tennis and golf. It might be beneficial initially to teach the youngster to paddle on only one side of the canoe (whichever is her more comfortable side), letting others in the canoe alternate sides for paddling and controlling direction. The child will probably enjoy the rhythm of paddling, and singing a song to help her maintain a good rhythm might also be beneficial, and fun. A well-fitted life jacket is an absolute must – ideally one of the newer thin, vest styles that will not impede her arm motion.

○ A truly wonderful sport for the adolescent or teen with NLD is kayaking. Of course, this assumes that your child is a proficient swimmer. The NLD child's deficits don't seem to affect them at all with this particular sport. There is no crossing midline, since the paddle is one long bar with a paddle on either end. She would propel herself by simply rotating her arms, using the same motion as her legs do when pedaling a bicycle. Also, she sits within the hull of the kayak, rather than sitting up high as in a canoe. Therefore, your youngster is likely to respond to the craft as an extension of her body, rather than feeling like she is going to topple over. A single person kayak allows the youngster to be in total control, and can be quite liberating, providing the child with a good boost to her self-esteem. Again, a well-fitted life vest which does not impede her arm movements is highly recommended. A word of caution – no 'white water' kayaking until the youngster is extremely proficient at the sport – ponds will do quite nicely for quite some time.

OTHER ACTIVITIES

The following are additional activities which may interest your NLD child:

○ for children who have a dog, agility training or obedience training;

○ ping pong (table tennis);

○ croquet;

○ track and field (especially in the middle and high school years);

○ tetherball (a soccer-sized ball attached by a length of rope to a small pole);

○ karate or tae kwon do.

If your child would like to participate in a team sport, she may do best with volleyball. The rules are rather straightforward, and there isn't a lot of running around. However, because of the inherent difficulties with team sports, it might be wise to wait until your child is a bit older before attempting a competitive team sport – possibly late middle to high school.

EARLY INTERVENTION

Although these children may never be a star in team sports, there are many things that they can excel at. However, if we're going to help these youngsters, we need to start very simply, gradually introducing new skills. So, let's start back at the beginning.

- If your child is young, use opportunities to improve her balance. Have her walk on a stable balance beam at ground level. Draw a chalk line down the driveway and make a game of walking the line without falling off, or draw parallel lines and walk between them without stepping over the line.

- Try and teach her to hop, skip, and jump. Once she has learned how to hop and skip, use sidewalk chalk to make an over-sized hopscotch grid on your driveway and teach her how to play the game, verbally scripting the rules.

- If she is unable to learn how to swing on a swing through verbal scripting, try standing behind her and put your arms on top of her legs. Move her legs back and forth to show her how to pump. When she understands the leg motion, you can probably script the rest with verbal cues, such as 'push' (legs straight out), 'pull' (legs back under the seat), or whatever words you choose, and chant it as she begins to pump her legs so that she develops a rhythm. Keep giving her a gentle push to keep up her momentum until she is able to create her own.

° There are two terrific types of balls that are great for these
  kids – Gertie and Bongo balls. Gertie balls are made of a
  very soft material that is exceptionally light. Bongo balls
  are outer cotton shells with large blown-up balloons
  inside. NLD children tend to really enjoy these two types
  of balls because they realize quite quickly that they can't
  be hurt by them. Balls such as these are easier for the child
  to try and catch because they are larger, very light, and
  don't require as much dexterity. The Gertie ball is also a
  good one to use to teach the child how to kick, for the
  same reasons that it is good for catching. If you don't have
  these specific types of balls where you live, think large,
  soft, and light.

° A great way to introduce catching a ball with a glove is
  with a ball that sticks to Velcro, and a glove with Velcro in
  the palm area. The child holds up her glove hand, and you
  throw the ball to the palm area, and she catches it – the
  ball actually stuck to the Velcro in the glove. Watch that
  little face light up!

° For initial ball and bat activity, a substantially oversized
  plastic bat, and lightweight plastic ball, such as a large
  whiffle ball (a softball-sized hollow white plastic ball with
  holes in it), are good choices. The larger the bat surface,
  the better chance that it will make contact with the ball. As
  with any youngster, it is easiest to teach them how to
  swing the bat by standing behind them with your arms
  around them, both of you holding the bat.

° A great exercise for hand–eye coordination is that little
  paddle with the ball attached by a long elastic. Trying to
  bounce the ball against the paddle may be difficult, but
  will probably be fun if the child has already developed
  some level of hand–eye coordination.

° When introducing the child to a tricycle, experiment with
  both a traditional tricycle and a big wheel (the one with a
  big front wheel, where the seat is set back, and the child's

legs are stretched out in front of her to reach the pedals). One type of trike may work better than the other since the pedaling pressure is a bit different for each. With a traditional tricycle the child is pushing down, and with the big wheel she is pushing forward in order to pedal. If she has difficulty understanding how to pedal through verbal scripting, then you might try the same method as with the swing. Stand behind her, with your arms on the top of her legs, rotating them to demonstrate the pedaling motion. Once the child learns to manage a tricycle, it may be quite some time before she is able to master a two-wheeled bicycle, but what's the rush?

○ Another thought is to introduce the child to a scooter. She may have less difficulty learning to propel herself with a scooter than with a bicycle. This only requires that one leg moves while the other remains stationary, rather than coordinating the motion of both legs.

A FEW FINAL THOUGHTS

Pogo sticks, unicycles, stilts, and the like are not recommended for NLD children. Tree houses may be safer if built under, rather than in, the tree. If your child is young, and you have a swing set or playscape, remove the lower rungs on ladders so that she can't climb them, then finding herself unable to get down. These children will, in all likelihood, not have an appreciation of the danger of heights and the fact that jumping from a high ledge or window into a pile of leaves will probably get her a broken neck.

Finally, invest in well-fitting shoes. Consider 'high top' sneakers, as the child may benefit from the additional ankle support which the higher shoe provides. Many NLD children have a problem with pronated arches (flat feet). If your youngster has this problem, see an orthopedist to determine whether or not orthopedic inserts are necessary for sports – or for all activities for that matter.

SUMMARY
Coordination

- ° NLD youngsters are uncoordinated, seem to trip and/or fall a lot, and may have an awkward gait.

- ° Spatial, psychomotor, and nonverbal problem solving deficits all play a role in the child's coordination difficulties.

Team sports

- ° Game rules are confusing, noise creates additional stress and social demands make the entire exercise overwhelming.

- ° Volleyball may be the best team sport, but should probably wait until late middle or high school.

Individual sports

- ° As with all things, sports and other physical pursuits need to be taught verbally in a step-by-step fashion.

- ° Private instruction is recommended, at least when first learning a new sport, and instructors may be found through Special Olympics.

- ° Individual sports which are well-suited for the NLD child include:

    swimming; skating; tennis; golf; archery; horse-back riding; canoeing; kayaking; dog agility/ obedience; ping pong; croquet; track and field; tetherball; karate; tae kwon do.

- ° Provide appropriate safety equipment and shoes with excellent support.

Early intervention

- Teach the child how to hop, skip, and jump. Gertie and Bongo balls are good for catching and kicking, a Velcro glove for catching. A large plastic bat and light plastic ball may work well. A paddle with an attached ball is good hand-eye exercise.

- Swinging may require that you move the child's legs with your hands to show her the motion.

- Riding a tricycle or bicycle may come late for the child. Consider a traditional tricycle or a big wheel, whichever is easier for the child. Scooters require only one leg to work, while the other remains stationary.

Chapter 7

Managing the Environment

As the title of this chapter indicates, the following pages will deal with managing the NLD child's environment. Before going further, however, there is something that you should know:

1. The single most important thing that you can do for your child is to provide her with the right environment.

2. The single most important thing that you can do for your child is to provide her with the right environment.

3. The single most important thing that you can do for your child is to provide her with the right environment.

As the saying goes…three times for the normal mind. Since this is such a critically important point, it seemed appropriate to begin this chapter by placing significant emphasis on the issue.

It might be helpful to clarify what is meant by 'environment' as it is addressed in this chapter and referred to in other sections of this book. We are not talking the sun, moon, stars, smog, or ozone problems. The definition of the NLD child's environment is much narrower and more immediate. It refers to the setting, surroundings, and conditions which are often difficult for the child. Environmental stressors may include noise, lights, crowds, fast-paced social interactions and unstructured activities such as school recess, parties and other celebrations.

In this chapter, we will discuss the type of environment which the child needs, and how environmental demands may result in the erroneous conclusion that the NLD child has a behavior problem. Since the child has tremendous difficulty in processing the demands of a world that she does not understand and finds overwhelming, we must first create an appropriate environment for her, and then teach her how to adapt an environment to better meet her needs. Issues which relate specifically to the safety of the NLD child are covered in the final chapter of this book.

Family members and others probably can't, or won't, appreciate the tremendous difficulty that your child has in processing her environment, coping with external stimuli, shifting mental set (shifting from her agenda to yours, or from one task to another), and the host of other challenges that both exhaust and overwhelm her. Creating the right environment for your child is not coddling, although you may be accused of that – it is absolutely critical to her ability to function.

THE NEED FOR PREDICTABILITY

You have no doubt read and heard many times that these children hate surprises, and thrive on routine. What we might consider boring – doing the same thing, the same way, day in and day out – the NLD child finds comforting. Because she has so much difficulty processing her world, it completely exhausts her. She needs as much predictability as possible in order to get through the day without becoming totally overwhelmed.

Many of us live with our NLD children's temper tantrums, meltdowns, and rages – call them what you will. There is a direct correlation between the child's meltdowns and our unrealistic expectations of them, the complexity of their environment, or both. Although an older child may actually be able to 'manage' a difficult environment for an extended period of time, at some point it will become too much.

It is essential to understand that these kids have no filtering mechanism to block out extraneous stimuli. Everything comes at them with equal force – noise, lights, images, people – and they are virtually bombarded with information that they are unable to sort, discarding the irrelevant and acting on the relevant. This has to be done for them, by creating a world in which they can function, not one in which we or others wish they could. A dear friend, Liane Willey, captured it so well when she said, 'It's like they need sunglasses for their brain.' Exactly!

It is difficult to imagine what the world is really like for the NLD child. One of the most complex settings is school, so we will look at how that environment might affect the child. First, they go to school on a bus, where there are all of those seats, and no understanding of which one to choose, and no friend to sit with. During the drive, there are all of the mechanical noises that the bus makes, along with the chatter of 70 other children. Are the noises something to worry about? Are they normal? What are the children talking about? Why are they talking so loudly, and throwing things around? What are the rules?

Then, when the bus arrives at school, still more chaos as hundreds of children pour out of various buses, chattering, yelling, and shoving, and all seeming to know where to go. The anxiety is building as the child wends her way through the maze of children and hallways to find her classroom. She puts away her things, and sits at her desk. The lights are so bright, the noise extreme as the other children are putting away their possessions, chattering and laughing, chairs scraping the floor as they get ready to start their day.

The day has barely begun, and for the spatially challenged child, just getting to class was exhausting. The child with auditory sensitivity is already suffering, and those with sensitivity to bright light want to close their eyes. The rules are a mystery – so many children misbehaving on the bus, and in the classroom they seem like a herd of wild animals. When all of the noise stops abruptly, she doesn't understand that it is because the teacher has entered the room, and that is the cue to behave.

The overwhelmed NLD youngster puts her head on her desk and covers it with her arms. The teacher thinks that the student's parents are not seeing that the child gets enough sleep, or that she hasn't had breakfast, or is misbehaving, or any one of a number of erroneous assumptions. The fact is that the child is already utterly exhausted, and she knows that it will be many, many more hours before she is allowed to return home.

If the sensory and environmental issues weren't enough, the child is unable to anticipate what will happen next. Most of us have the ability to be flexible. We develop an awareness of 'if this, then that' which allows us to handle most change. We know what the likely outcome will be when faced with a set of circumstances, and based on our prior experience with similar situations. NLD children have a great deal of difficulty generalizing – meaning that they are unable to apply prior experiences to the situation at hand. Therefore, for them, most situations that they are faced with are new, and they don't know what to expect or what to do.

Consider for a moment the situations that we are unable to readily adapt to – the death of a loved one, a divorce, a job change, or a move to a new place. These situations are traumatic to us because we don't have enough experience with any of these events to develop coping strategies. We may respond to each of these situations in various ways – from anxiety, to panic, to withdrawal, to depression. Now consider the world of the NLD child:

○ they do not understand that a situation which they are faced with may be similar to one they have experienced in the past;

○ because they do not see situations as similar, they are unable to develop an experiential base of information to pull from and apply when faced with a 'new' situation;

○ they do not have the ability to anticipate what may occur when faced with a 'new' situation.

Between environmental stressors and the child's inability to generalize and anticipate what will occur, is it any wonder that she is continually overwhelmed and exhausted? Is it any wonder that she has 'meltdowns' or temper tantrums? How well could you handle the equivalent of the death of a parent, a divorce, a move to a new place, and a job change in a week, or even in a day? This is what it is like for the NLD child, and this is why we must provide them with as much predictability as possible.

It is incumbent on us to simplify and structure the NLD child's environment so that she is better able to get through the day without becoming overwhelmed. Only then can we teach her how to identify what situations are difficult for her, and what strategies are helpful in reducing stress. At some point, she will be living on her own and will need to know how to create an environment which is appropriate for her needs.

MANAGING MULTIPLE ENVIRONMENTS

A complicating factor in providing an appropriate environment for the NLD child is the high percentage of households where both parents work. This invariably creates a situation where the child, who has difficulty coping in a single environment, is required to manage in multiple environments. This creates additional stress on the NLD child, and subsequently on the entire family. For a preschool-age child whose parents work, she is required to manage two environments – her home as well as a daycare setting. This is quite difficult, and if the daycare setting is large, the child does not have the skill to cope in such a complex setting, let alone the ability to manage two settings. For the school-age child of working parents, the child must manage at least three separate settings – school, daycare for before and after school, and her own home. If she participates in after-school activities, the problem is that much more difficult. Although daycare may be required for both the younger and older child, care must be given to the setting.

If your child needs to be cared for while both parents work, it is far better to have her provided for through in-home daycare. This can either be in the child's home or in the caregiver's home. When interviewing caregivers, it would be wise to select an individual and a setting that is compatible with the child's home setting – similar rules, routines, expectations, and so forth. This will increase the likelihood that she will be able to cope without significant additional stress. However, it is important to understand that multiple settings are not the ideal situation for an NLD child. If she has to manage in several settings, you will probably see behaviors which reflect her frustration, stress and fatigue.

Unfortunately, the situation with multiple environments does not improve as the child gets older. In fact, it gets far more complex and stressful. As the expectations become greater, and the environment(s) more complex, her ability to manage will deteriorate. This is why you often see an NLD child 'hit the wall' in middle school. Let's look at the difference between the daily school environments of a grammar school versus a middle school.

The younger child is in one classroom for most of the day, with the same classmates and teacher. When they have 'specials' (art, music, library, and so forth), the students attend them as a group, and if they physically move from one room to the next, the teacher accompanies them. In this type of situation, the NLD child often learns to function fairly well, unless she has multiple environments outside of school, the combination of which makes her world too complex.

Once the child enters middle school, the expectations are far greater, and her environment is infinitely more difficult. Let's take a look at what the average middle school demands are for the NLD child. One teacher and one class are replaced with different teachers for each subject, which averages about seven teachers per day. Rather than one group of students there are now a different group of students in each class, again averaging seven classes per day. A simple daily schedule is replaced with an alternating day or alternating week schedule. The student is required to move from classroom to classroom on her own, while navigating corridors crowded with students every 50 minutes or so.

It's a wonder that neurologically typical children are able to handle the stress of middle school. Clearly, the complexity of this environment is inappropriate for NLD youngsters. However, since we can't all homeschool our children, or enroll them in private schools, it is important to teach the child how to manage as effectively as possible, and limit, or eliminate entirely, any environments other than home and school.

So how do we teach the child how to identify her needs, what overwhelms her, and manage in an environment as complex as middle school? Ideally, it starts when the child is very young. First, we must have an awareness of her environmental challenges, and create a home environment that is appropriate for her needs. Gradually, we introduce and teach strategies that allow the child to cope effectively.

Schedules

Long before we can begin to teach the child to identify her needs, or what overwhelms her, we must first introduce her to the concept of a schedule. As early as possible, we need to provide her with a predictable routine. If the child is quite young, we simply provide a routine with as little disruption as possible. She gets up in the morning, and goes to bed at night, at around the same time each day. There is an order in which things are done – eat breakfast, brush teeth, get dressed – and the sequence is always the same. We explain to the child when she gets up – 'Time for breakfast!' Once complete, we tell her about the next activity – 'We're done with breakfast, so it's time to brush our teeth!' Through repetition and verbal scripting, she will learn her daily routine. However, you should give considerable thought to whatever the schedule will be, because once it is learned, the child will resist any change to it.

Transitions

Transitions of any kind are difficult for this child, and may well include difficulty in transitioning to wakefulness, as well as to sleep. If this is the case with your child, then it is wise to incorporate steps in her routine that allow for this problem. For instance, if she is required to get up at 7:20am, you could wake her at 7:00am, and let her know that it is almost time to get up. At 7:15am you would tell her that she has five more minutes (although she might not have a concept of time, she will quickly learn that this is not very long). Finally, at 7:20am you would tell her that it is now time to get out of bed.

Similar steps can be incorporated into her bedtime routine to assist her in transitioning to sleep. For instance, you start the routine with a notice that it's 'x' minutes (or possibly one TV show) before bedtime. When the time is up, you then take her to brush her teeth, go to the bathroom, and then you tuck her into bed. You tell her that you will read one story, and then it's lights out. If your child is older and she doesn't yet have an established routine, develop one with her input.

These routines will become rituals which provide predictability. Your child will depend on her routine, so be consistent – if you're not, be prepared for tantrums with the little ones, and acting out behavior with the older child. All children benefit from this type of consistency, but for NLD youngsters it is absolutely critical – it is reassuring and comforting.

When introducing the child to a new environment where she will be spending an extended period of time (for example school), provide her with a simple map of the building. Draw arrows from the front door to her destination. Practice walking the route several times before the child has to do it alone. Until the child is familiar with the route, put a copy of the map in her pocket or in her school binder.

Allow plenty of time

The more routine there is to the day, the less anxious and frustrated the child will be. However, in addition to providing a routine, it is also important to allow plenty of time for her to do what needs doing. Expect that everything will take this child longer, and understand that if she is rushed she is far less able, and far more likely to fly into a rage. Even if you are tempted to allow her to sleep a few minutes longer in the morning, resist. It is easier for her to get up at the normal time, and go through her routine at the pace that she is accustomed to. Also remember that she has only one pace. Telling her to hurry up is fruitless – she truly can't adjust her pace, and will become frustrated by your prodding.

It is also important to have a consistent schedule for the remainder of the day – lunch at a specific time (or after a particular event), snack at a predictable time, supper, bath, and so forth. Any change to the routine should be explained to the child before it occurs. For instance, if you are taking her somewhere on Tuesday, you would explain on Monday evening that tomorrow, after we get dressed – or whatever consistent event takes place every day which occurs just before you are going to leave – we are going to the Smith's house so that I can visit with Mary and you can play with Susie. We will come home to eat lunch. You are preparing her for a change in routine, explaining what you will be doing, and for approximately how long.

The concept of time

For an older child, you can be more specific with times, but the concept of time is difficult for these children, so concrete events that 'mark' a time of day may be useful for several years. She is far more apt to understand the duration of an hour, by explaining that it is the same amount of time as her favorite television show. Timers and watches with an alarm are also helpful. If something is to occur in an hour, and she needs to know when 60 minutes has elapsed, set a timer for her, or buy her a watch with an alarm on it, and set it for one hour.

Being able to tell time will, in all likelihood, come much later for these children than for their peers, and analog devices may only confuse her. If your child is anxious to know how to tell time, and is not grasping time with an analog device, try a digital watch.

Forewarning and cueing

Prepare the child for everything from suppertime to guests. NLD children react very badly to unexpected events. They also have tremendous challenges in 'shifting mental set' – meaning that once the child is focused on something, moving her attention to something else is quite difficult for her. Forewarning and cueing are helpful strategies. If she is engrossed in an activity, and it is getting close to mealtime, let her know that she will have to stop in five minutes. Timers are also helpful for this. Tell her that the timer will go off when five minutes has elapsed, and then she will have to stop what she is doing and come to dinner.

If you are expecting company, let the child know early on who is coming, when they are arriving, how long they will stay, and what, if anything, will be expected of her while the guests are at your home. In order to increase the likelihood of your child handling visitors appropriately, suggest to your friends that they call before coming, rather than just dropping in.

Eating out

If you are planning to eat out at a restaurant with your NLD child, do some advance planning. Go to the restaurant ahead of time to determine if you think your child can handle the environment, and if there is something on the menu that she will enjoy. If you can make a reservation, explain that your child has difficulty with noise, and ask for the quietest table.

For the young child (and maybe for the not so young child as well), even if you think there is something on the menu that she will like, bring something from home just in case – the menu selection might not be prepared to her liking, or may not be what she expected. If you have brought something with you for her to eat, you will all be able to enjoy your meal without a tantruming child forcing you to leave. Do understand that the child isn't simply being a brat – she is in a strange place, with lots of environmental stimuli, and no understanding that not all grilled-cheese sand-wiches are created equal.

Anticipate what could go wrong. Expect problems such as spilled milk, and don't become upset. The more composed the adults are, the calmer the child will be. If you anticipate problems, you will be less likely to get angry, or feel that your outing has been spoiled. In other words, prepare for the worst, and hope for the best.

Shopping

It is unrealistic to think that the NLD child will enjoy excursions to the supermarket or mall. These are overwhelming environments for her, and if required to go, she will probably react quite poorly.

Try to manage your schedule so that the child can be left at home with your partner, or some other familiar caregiver when the time comes to run errands or do your weekly grocery shopping. Naturally, there will be occasions when you must take the child with you – either because there is no one to care for her, or because she needs to be fitted for shoes or the like. Be kind to yourself and your child by selecting a small store, shop when it is apt to be the least crowded, and accomplish your task as quickly as possible.

Although you may be tempted to take your child with you to buy her clothes, it may be more realistic to be her 'personal shopper' when at all possible. It is far easier to return what doesn't work out than to expect the child to cooperate while trying on various outfits in an environment that overwhelms her. Also, since many of these children like as much consistency in their clothing as they do in their routine, shopping for them may be a matter of buying the same sweatpants and T-shirts in various colors. As the child gets older, and may be more difficult to fit, taking her with you may be necessary. Select the smallest store, go at the quietest time, and if an inducement will help, then by all means, go for it!

Since these children become so dependent on their auditory system, they may have acute hearing. Loud noises both in and outside the home may be difficult for the child to tolerate. Always give her warning when you can – if you are going to turn on the vacuum, give her the option of going to her room before turning it on. Do the same before mowing the lawn, or any other activity with a noise component that may be bothersome to the child. Naturally, you can't totally control all noise. Consider getting earplugs for her to use when the noise level becomes too invasive. If this proves to be an effective strategy, it might be beneficial to have custom-fitted earplugs made by an audiologist. They aren't terribly expensive, and are far more comfortable than those that are sold at the pharmacy. And take the earplugs with you whenever you are taking the child somewhere noisy such as a store, restaurant or amusement park.

When you are out and about, or at any other time when the child may become overwhelmed by external stimuli, another option is a portable cassette or CD player with headphones. It is hard to say at what age this will be effective, but at some point it is likely to become her method of choice to block out the world. There are a variety of headphone styles, so there is sure to be one that your child will accept. If she doesn't like the feel of it rubbing against her hair, consider having her wear a baseball cap with the headphones worn over it. Select either stories or music, whichever she prefers.

The bedroom

Whether you have one child, or several, the NLD child should have her own bedroom. This may create a hardship, but it is very important, and every effort should be made to accommodate this need. This child requires a lot of quiet time where she can be alone to relax from the daily demands and stress of managing in a world she doesn't understand, and which exhausts her. Her room will become her refuge – her safe place where there are no demands and no expectations. Allow her the freedom of decorating it the way that she wants. She may prefer bold colors versus the pastels that you would have chosen. Help her create a sanctuary that is truly hers and insist that her siblings honor her space and privacy, and she theirs. Never give her room to visiting guests, as this is when she most needs her quiet, safe place.

Parties and holidays

Special occasions in our lives are likely the most stressful events for our NLD children. Birthdays, Christmas, Hanukkah, and similar holidays, should be handled based on what the child can handle, rather than on our own festive preference. Celebrating a birthday with immediate family is more than enough for the young child. This is not a child who will enjoy a birthday party where all her classmates are invited to go bowling. Besides the environmental issues, she is likely not coordinated enough to even enjoy bowling. In the middle elementary grades, a birthday party with just a few children will be as much as the child can handle without becoming over-stimulated or overwhelmed and acting inappropriately. If family members want to participate in the birthday celebration, two separate small parties (one for school friends and one for family) would almost certainly be more successful than one large one. Keep both parties limited to two hours or less, erring on the less side for the younger child, and have them on separate days.

By late elementary school, and certainly by middle school, she may want to have a sleepover. Keep the number of invited guests to a minimum – say three other girls – and structure the activities. A nice plan might be for the children to arrive at 7:00pm. You can take them to an early evening movie, followed by a trip to the pizza parlor before returning home for cake. After the cake, allow the child to open her gifts. It should now be around 11:00pm and time for the girls to wash up, brush their teeth, and get into their pajamas. Have a video on hand for them to watch while they are tucked into their sleeping bags on the floor, and provide snacks and drinks while they enjoy their video. Tell them that lights out is at whatever time you determine, and when it's time for lights out, let them know. As with all young girls, they will likely be whispering into the wee hours. In this way you can hope to provide enough structure for your NLD child to get through the night without acting inappropriately. If you see inappropriate behavior, it is almost certain that she is over-stimulated. Quietly call her away from her friends, and give her a few moments to compose herself before returning to the party. Don't expect perfection, but try and avoid a situation where your child will embarrass herself. By being vigilant through the night, you won't get much sleep, but the social experience for your child will be worth it.

Without a doubt, one of the most difficult months of the year for NLD children is December, especially if they are of school age. The child's normally quiet home is disrupted – furniture may be moved to accommodate a Christmas tree and decorations are everywhere, so that nothing looks the same. Other children find all of this exhilarating, but for the NLD child it may be quite threatening – her security of sameness is gone. There is shopping for presents, wrapping packages, baking seasonal foods and scheduling changes. In school, there are seasonal plays, assemblies and scheduling changes. Her classmates are likely to be quite exuberant in anticipation of both the holidays and winter recess, and quite a handful for the teachers to control. Is it any wonder that the NLD child is overwhelmed and out of sorts?

It is important to explain to the child the purpose of the holiday celebrations so that she has some context in which to understand the goings on. Involving the child in the process of decorating the house, and doing it over a period of time, is important so that the change isn't abrupt and jolting. Develop rituals that the child can look forward to from year to year. If you are Christian, baking a birthday cake for baby Jesus would be more meaningful and enjoyable for your child than disrupting the kitchen for days baking dozens of Christmas cookies. Try to look at the holidays through her eyes, modify the daily routine as little as possible, and enjoy the season in simple and meaningful ways.

Involving the child

As more is expected of the older child, such as when she enters middle school, the early teaching which you have done should be applied to her school environment. It is important to involve the child in the process of how to modify the environment or schedule in a way that is easier for her to manage. Remember, she needs to understand what is difficult and causes stress so that eventually she will be able to make modifications to her environment on her own. If she finds the cafeteria too overwhelming, then you can discuss her difficulty in these types of situations and consider alternatives that may be effective, such as eating in the classroom or elsewhere. If she finds the corridors during class changes too difficult to navigate with all of the other students, you may arrange to have her change classes a few minutes before the other students. If she is unable to handle the number of teachers assigned to her, an option may be to drop some of her 'specials' (art, music, and so forth).

This chapter opened with the statement that the single most important thing that you can do for your child is to provide her with the right environment. You have now read many reasons as to why this is so, and have seen others in your own personal situation. It takes thought and planning to provide your child with a safe, manageable environment. As you implement strategies, tell her why you are doing so, and what the consequences might be if you don't. Remember, she needs to hear the logic in order to learn. Explain the benefits of wearing earplugs to block out the noise, or limit the size of a party so that she doesn't become overwhelmed and embarrass herself by acting inappropriately. The point is to teach her what works, so that she will eventually be able to do this for herself.

SUMMARY

There is a direct correlation between the child's melt-downs and the complexity of her environment and/or our unrealistic expectations of her. Multiple environments are incredibly difficult for her to manage. She requires predictability, a consistent routine, and a refuge. Provide her with her own bedroom.

Allow her plenty of time to do things such as get dressed, or organize her backpack for school. She has only one pace, and if prodded to rush, she may become confused and unable to perform. Forewarning and cueing are good strategies to prepare a child for a change in agenda from hers to yours. Provide a map of a new environment such as school, and practice walking the route she will take to and from class. The concept of time is something that she may not understand. Use timers and consider a digital watch with an alarm.

Plan ahead for eating out and shopping. Consider being your child's 'personal shopper' rather than taking her to a store or a mall where she may become overwhelmed. Parties and holidays may be overwhelming for the child. Keep guests to a minimum, and tone down the celebration. Use earplugs or a portable CD player with headphones if your child is overwhelmed.

We must instill structure and teach the child to know her own needs, to be able to identify when she is overwhelmed and by what, as well as how to reorder her world so that she can function as independently as possible. It isn't easy, and it will take many years, but it can be accomplished, and that is our goal.

Chapter 8

Organization

You will quickly find that order is a necessity for your NLD child. These children thrive on a tidy room and home. Clutter for her is a world of chaos. Remember her spatial problems – she is apt to bump into, or fall over, things that are out of place. Also, because of her visual processing difficulties, she is far less likely to find something if her visual field is cluttered, even if the object that she is looking for is right under her nose.

ORGANIZATION AT HOME

The child's visual perception difficulties probably cause her far more problems than we might realize. You may be familiar with the following scenario since it happens all too often. You send the child to her bedroom to get her shoes. She marches off as instructed, but by the time she gets to her bedroom, she's forgotten what you asked her to do. She calls to you, and asks you to repeat the instruction, which you do. She then enters her bedroom with toys, clothes, and bedding thrown helter-skelter. She can't 'see' the shoes on the floor amid the other items strewn about. Back she comes without the shoes, telling you that she couldn't find them. You know they are there, because you saw them on the floor not five minutes ago. Now you both march off to her bedroom to find the shoes. There they are in the middle of the floor right where you last saw them. You're annoyed, you point, and say, 'They're right THERE!' The already frustrated child is now getting anxious because you've raised your voice to her. She has no clue where there is, and shouts, 'WHERE?' Unfortunately, we're all human, and depending on your frustration level, you might shout, 'Right in the middle of the floor – are you blind?' The fact is, that in this situation, she is blind. She truly can't isolate the shoes amid the cluttered visual field.

There are a couple of other options that would be far less stressful for both of you. You could literally walk the child through finding her shoes, but this assumes that you are standing right there – 'Take three steps forward and stop; bend down; put your right hand down on the floor; move it toward the bed; and there they are!' However, it would be better still if she could find her shoes on the first trip to the bedroom without a hitch. Creating this level of independence requires tremendous organization, not only of the bedroom, but of the entire house. A good thing – but for those of you who are totally disorganized, you'll hate this chapter!

Organizing the house for your NLD child not only means less frustration and fewer 'meltdowns' for the child, but it is also starting her on the way toward learning the organizational skills necessary for her future success and self-sufficiency. Your home is a microcosm of the child's world, and represents many of the challenges that she will face outside the home. Providing her with the strategies to function well at home is an important developmental process that will help her to function in a world that is utterly overwhelming.

It begins with organization – lots of organization. This really needs to begin at a young age, because it won't be long before the child won't allow you to move anything! These children find a tremendous amount of security in sameness. So, start now, and involve her in the organizing process, especially in her bedroom.

The remainder of this chapter covers organizational ideas that you may find helpful. Use the ones that work, discard the others, and incorporate your own solutions.

Storage

These children don't adapt well to the use of a toy box. Although it's great for putting toys away – everything just gets thrown in – it's a nightmare for them to try and find a toy. It's no surprise – in the same way that she couldn't find her shoes on the bedroom floor, a toy box with everything thrown together makes it impossible for her to 'see' what she wants. So, she tosses the toys out one by one until she finds the particular item she is looking for. Yes, most children do the same thing, but for NLD children, they have no other means of finding what they are looking for when it is mixed in with so many other objects.

Instead of a single large toy box, try using smaller containers (from shoe-box size to cartons), storing like things together. It might be a good idea to label the boxes in some way; either with words, or by some color system, so that the child knows what is where, and can find her toys by herself. Plastic milk crates that you can see through are excellent for this purpose, and come in various sizes. As you organize the child's possessions, have her help you. Let her put things together that she sees as similar. For the young ones, in addition to teaching organization, you are also fostering the application of similarities and categories. These are basic, important concepts to develop in NLD children, since they don't naturally think in terms of grouping. Let her enjoy the process rather than making it a chore. Organizational skills are a weakness for these kids, so it is wise to be patient as they develop their skills, or they may become frustrated and give up. Guide them and help them as they need it, but let them do what they can.

Organize collections

Most, if not all, of these kids tend to be natural collectors. Encourage these types of hobbies, such as collecting trading cards, rocks, action figures, whatever interests the child. She will probably be quite receptive to organizing her 'treasures,' which will further develop rudimentary organizational skills. Help her with this, and give her some ideas as to how she might organize. If she collects trading cards, they could be organized in binders, in small boxes, or in special boxes made specifically for this purpose – whatever seems to strike her fancy. Talk out the advantages to each, so that the child understands each option, and then makes her choice. Once she has selected the medium, help her sort and organize her collection, possibly making labels for each item. Remember, this exercise is difficult for her, and she can easily become overwhelmed. However, she will probably respond quite well to order and structure and welcome your efforts to help her with these types of activities. Taking the time to teach the child early organizational skills will make it easier to later teach her how to apply these skills to her school activities and assignments.

Shelves and cubbies

The ideal arrangement in the child's bedroom is to eliminate drawers as much as possible, using shelves and cubbies instead. Milk crates come in handy here as well. For some items of clothing, such as her undergarments and socks, you will probably want to use drawers. However, for the remainder of her clothes, use shelves or cubbies, and keep everything organized. This approach to storage allows her to see what it is that she is looking for, without trying to remember which drawer it may be in. Even if the child is young, start the process, so that gradually you can explain where everything is, and that everything has a place. Try to avoid hanging garments on hangers. If something needs to be hung, such as her bathrobe – use a big hook! Remember always to put the same pieces of clothing in the same drawer, shelf, or cubby, otherwise it is unlikely that she will learn where to find them as she becomes more independent.

Organizing clothes

Organize the child's clothes with the intent that, at some point, *she* will be selecting what she wants to wear. Decide if it makes more sense to put all the pants together, and all the shirts together, or if clothing should be stored by outfit instead. If stored by outfit, you might want to clip everything together, right down to the socks. Or, you can keep it simple, and buy clothes that are inter-changeable. Remember that we want the child to look nice, so it would be helpful to avoid the possibility of her putting on a striped shirt with plaid pants. We want to foster independence and self-help skills. Chastising her for putting the striped shirt with the plaid pants will not increase self-reliance. Buy clothes with this issue in mind, so that if she grabs any old thing, at least it will match. This issue may actually be moot if your child has sensitivity to clothing. Her entire wardrobe may consist of sweatpants and sweatshirts, or something similar, in varying colors. If so, consider yourself ahead of the game!

Hooks versus hangers

An early task that many of us try and teach our children is to hang up their coat. However, don't expect the NLD child to be able to hang her coat on a hanger. If she has, or had, trouble with buttons and zippers, she will certainly have difficulty getting a coat or jacket on a hanger. Even if she can wrestle the coat onto a hanger, it would probably fall off before making it into the closet. Rather than using a closet for the child's outerwear, put up hooks or use a coat tree, and make sure that the child can reach high enough to hang her coat on a hook without help. Ideally, the hook should be right by the door that she uses in order to come into the house and go outside, large enough to make it easy for her to put her coat on, and not crowded with everyone else's coats so that she can't find her own hook. You could make it even easier for her if the hooks or coat tree are for kids only – parents use the closet. Once the hook is up, or you have a coat tree, the first thing you do whenever she comes indoors is to remind her – 'Take off your jacket... now put it on the hook.' When it's time to go outside, even if she hasn't mastered getting her jacket or coat on by herself, she can fetch it from the hook. You'll be surprised at how quickly she adapts to this routine.

Closets

By six, seven, or eight, try removing the closet door(s) in your child's bedroom. Some of these children truly forget what is not visible to them, so removing the door can be quite helpful. However, the young ones might be frightened by the shadows in and around a closet without a door, hence the suggestion to wait awhile. The closet can be organized with shelves, cubbies, and a hook or two, and both her clothes and toys can be stored there. Keep the clutter to a minimum so that the visual field isn't overwhelming. Not only will she be more independent in finding toys to play with, but she will also be more able to put her things away when it is time to clean up.

If there isn't enough room to store her toys in the closet, you might organize them in boxes or various-sized milk crates which are then stored under her bed. Or, her toys can be stored on shelves, along with her books and smaller treasures. The idea here is organization, reduced clutter, and a system that will allow her to put her own things away – toys when younger, and clothes as she gets older.

Dos and don'ts

You may find yourself in a 'spring cleaning' mood one day, and decide to clean your NLD child's bedroom. By the time you're done, your back is killing you, but you have a terrific sense of accomplishment. The child comes home from school to a wonderfully clean room (wonderful to you, at least), and promptly goes bonkers. Without getting into the argument that erupts between you and your child, let's look at the problem.

What looks so nice and orderly to you seems like total chaos to her. You've *moved* things, and now she doesn't know where her possessions are, and can't *see* them. Her refuge has been violated, and it's all your fault! The safer approach is to involve the child in the process. When she is quite young, she can certainly help you put things away. As she gets a bit older, she will be capable of putting her toys away without help. Later still, she can be responsible for putting her own clothes away. It is critically important to the NLD child that her bedroom continues to be a safe haven, and remains consistent in all things. The best way to ensure that is to have her help put things in their proper place, or put things away by herself.

Ideally, create a routine where it isn't likely that her bedroom will get terribly messy. When her clothes come off at night, they go right into the hamper. Even a toddler can do that after you've changed them, so it's never too young to start! When she has finished playing with toys, the toys are put away. Make these activities consistent, and it will become a habit. When the room needs a thorough cleaning, include the child with age-appropriate tasks. Never, EVER, move her bedroom furniture around without her involvement. Remember, these kids do not handle change well, and surprising her by disrupting her refuge may have you up until 3:00am putting everything back to where it was.

More about hooks

Now to the bathroom, and a pet peeve. The use of towel rods makes little sense. Towels thrown carelessly over a rod probably causes more marital discord than the top being left off the tube of toothpaste! Face it – it's a nuisance to fold a towel and place it neatly over a rod, even for neatniks. With NLD children, it is almost impossible to perform what we think of as a simple task. Here's another place to use those hooks. Remove all those dastardly towel rods, and replace them with big hooks instead. If you have difficulty finding large hooks, an alternative is to use hooks designed to hold back draperies – the ones that you install on the side of the window and are used for draperies like tiebacks are used for curtains. Just hang them on the wall vertically instead of horizontally, and voilà – a great towel hook! Not only will the change from towel rods to hooks make it easier for your NLD child to put her towel away by herself, it might just foster a bit of marital harmony as well.

Lists and reminders

In addition to organizing the environment, it is important to teach the child how to organize her routine. Lists and reminders are essential to help these children remember what they have to do as well as the order in which to do it. Naturally, this relates to an older child who can either read or follow symbols which represent tasks.

There will probably be different lists for different times of the day. The morning list (hung in a convenient spot) may look something like this:

> go to the bathroom
> go downstairs and eat breakfast
> go back upstairs
> brush your teeth
> get dressed
> brush your hair.

When she gets home from school, there may be another list with the activities for the remainder of the afternoon. You may choose to have a schedule with times, rather than just a list of activities. It might look something like this:

    3:15 – get home and have a snack (no TV)
    3:30 – do your homework
    4:30 – practice the piano
    5:00 – watch TV (Nickelodeon).

There may also be an evening schedule including what the child is allowed to do after supper, along with an outline of her nightly routine. Remember that it is the order that is so important for these kids. So, even if you don't necessarily care about times, be consistent with the order in which they are to do certain tasks, so that the routine becomes ingrained and automatic.

Post-Its

It is unfair to expect these children to remember a lot of things – just getting through the day is challenge enough. It is wiser to give her a written reminder in the form of a note. Those little Post-Its are wonderful for this – you can stick them on a schoolbook, or on the mirror, wherever it makes sense to remind her of something. It is particularly important to use written reminders for anything that relates to school. She is far more likely to forget something that she is supposed to do once she gets to school because it is a difficult environment for her to function in, and she may forget if the reminder is not in writing. You will know when this procedure is ingrained in your child when she starts leaving Post-It notes on *your* mirror!

ORGANIZATION FOR SCHOOL

Although this book addresses 'at home' issues, there are a few school-related organizational topics that warrant covering here.

This child is invariably confused about what will happen when, which makes the school environment somewhat threatening when she is young, and very threatening in the upper grades when there is a lot of daily change to manage. The child may be so focused on where she is supposed to be during the next period, and how to get there, that she forgets to write down her homework assignment. If she is required to use a locker for her books, remember the problem with visual fields. A locker is small, and crammed full of books, notebooks, jacket or coat, backpack, and her lunch bag or box. Finding what she needs for a particular class can be very frustrating to an already overwhelmed student. The following suggestions might help your child manage her school day better.

- Create a schedule of her day. For the young child, the schedule may consist of icons which represent certain activities, or word representations. In the early grades, the schedule will be fairly simple, because the child spends the majority of her day in one classroom. For the older child, there are many class changes to remember. For all age groups, once you have created the schedule, shrink it down on your computer before you print it out, or on a copier when you make copies. Cut the schedules to the small size, and clip a fresh copy to her backpack every day. Before the child leaves the house, have her put the schedule in her shirt or pants pocket.

  There are two purposes for these daily schedules. One is so that the child knows where to go when, and the other is for the teacher to mark any changes to the daily school routine on the child's copy of her schedule. Changes should be marked on the schedule first thing in the morning so that she has forewarning of any change to her school day. Any change, no matter how minor, should be indicated. For the older student, insert a full sized copy of her schedule in a plastic sleeve, and put it in her school binder. For the older child, it is imperative that she has a schedule, and if she loses the small copy, there is always the one in her binder. Naturally, you'll need the cooperation of the teachers to implement this approach effectively. You'll be surprised at how quickly your child begins to rely on her printed schedule.

○ A daily agenda book or planner is another critical item for this child to have. All assignments, both short-term and long-term, should be entered into the agenda book on a daily basis. For the young child, and for some older ones as well, the teacher should do this. The assignment should be clear enough so that you understand what it means, because the child will probably forget by the time she gets home from school. As the child gets older, she can be required to write her assignments in the agenda book, but it should be signed off by the teacher. If additional clarification is required, the teacher should have the child elaborate, or the teacher can do it for her. By high school, the routine should be so ingrained in the child that she should be able to handle this responsibility on her own. The only exception to this may be long-term projects which you may want the teacher to write out for you. Either you or the teacher will then have to 'chunk out' the project, and make individual entries in the child's agenda book so that she can manage the assignment.

○ To make it easier for the child to find something in her locker, it's a good idea to color-code her books and associated material such as folders. You can cover the textbook with a particular color of paper, mark it with a piece of colored tape, or use some other method that allows the child to quickly see which book she is looking for. It's also advantageous to provide the child with a large, three-ring binder that zips closed. Within the binder there can be heavy-gauge folders for each subject. If the folders don't come three-hole punched, simply use the heavy-duty three-hole punch at the office-supply store when you buy the folders, and punch holes in them before you leave the store. Each folder should be a separate color, corresponding to the color-code you used on her textbooks. In addition to the folders, also include paper, either spiral bound or loose, but also three-hole punched, and a simple map of the school. Insert a zippered pouch for pencils, pens, erasers, and so forth, which has holes so that it can be secured by the rings in the binder. The idea is to have in one place all of the things that she will need throughout her school day.

○ If you use folders for each subject (the younger child may only need one folder), create a procedure for managing her papers. The folders should have inside pockets on both sides. Papers that are to be turned in to the teacher (such as completed homework assignments) may go in the right pocket, and papers returned from the teacher might go in the left. Whatever procedure you implement, be consistent.

○ Remember that whatever organizational system you implement, the child will probably use it for many years. When you create a procedure, involve her in the process, and don't forget to script her through it. Let her pick the colors, but as you put everything together, talk through 'Green is for science because it reminds me of the grass and trees, so we'll use the green folder, and cover your science book with green paper.' Even though you are color-coding, don't forget to mark in large print what the subject area is. Naturally, there will be little modifications as the child's needs change, but the overall system will probably continue. So, if you find a folder or binder that really works well for your child, stock up.

Organization and organizational skills are incredibly important to the NLD child. If you start with the simple things, like organizing her toys and clothes, it won't be such a stretch when you begin to introduce organizational skills for school. Continuing to build on the child's organizational skills as she gets older should make the demands of middle and high school a bit more possible.

SUMMARY

- Organization is a necessity for the NLD child. Clutter makes it impossible for her to find anything, increases her stress and doesn't allow independence.

- Visual perception problems make 'seeing' what she is looking for quite difficult. Organize toys and possessions in small containers, such as milk crates or on shelves. Use shelves for clothing instead of bureau drawers, and hooks instead of hangers or towel rods. Clip outfits together or buy interchangeable clothing.

- Remove the closet doors in the child's room and fill it with shelves and cubbies for storing clothing and toys or other possessions. Use collections as a means of teaching the child organizational skills.

- Never rearrange the child's bedroom without her involvement. Your order may be her chaos. Involve the child in keeping her room tidy, gradually transferring more of the responsibility to her as she becomes more adept.

○ Lists and reminders help her organize her day and remember important things. Post-Its are very helpful for written reminders.

○ Create a schedule for the child's school routine. Make it small, and provide the child with a clean copy each day to put in her pocket. Have teachers mark scheduling changes on the child's copy first thing in the morning. For the older child, put a second, larger copy in her binder. Use a daily agenda or planner for homework assignments.

○ Color-code school books and related materials, use a three-ring binder that zips closed, include heavy-duty folders and teach the child a procedure for managing papers in the folders. Verbally script this organizational process. Be sure that everything that the child will need during her school day fits in the binder (except, of course, her books).

Chapter 9

Thinking Skills

When the NLD child is young, her deficits in critical thinking may not be apparent. This level of thinking is not generally expected until the child is at least eight years old, and probably a bit older than that. However, if she is to reach her full potential, and grow to be an independent adult, she needs to be engaged in active learning and critical thinking from the earliest possible age.

DECISIONS AND CHOICES

Decisions and choices are basic thinking skills which start at a very tender age. If you ask your toddler what she wants to eat, she tells you. Although it may not be what you will allow, she has an idea of what she likes and wants. When you ask an NLD child what she wants, she may not have an answer. The child may look at you with a blank expression, so you end up making the decision for her. However, if you ask her to choose between apple juice and grape juice, she will be more apt to respond. Making even a simple decision requires that you have a lot of information.

Even very young children have nonverbal information that allows them to make decisions that NLD children are unable to make. The neurologically typical child knows the food Mom generally has on hand, or has actually seen it in the refrigerator or cupboard. The NLD child doesn't realize that Mom expects her to intuit what the choices are. In addition, since visual processing is an area of deficit, these youngsters do not rely on that modality to store information. The deficit is even more pronounced when the visual field is cluttered, like a refrigerator or cupboard. So, since the child is unaware that she is supposed to intuit, and couldn't in any event since she didn't process what was in the refrigerator or cupboard, she doesn't have all of the information that she needs in order to make even a simple decision. Yes, it's often easier for us to make decisions on the child's behalf – just hand her a drink – but she needs to learn how to think, and we need to understand her deficits so that we can teach her how to think.

ACTIVE LEARNING

NLD youngsters don't have the learning advantages of their age mates, who process through visual and tactile modalities, through the exploration of their environment and through language. The NLD child's learning modality is limited primarily to language, which puts her at a huge disadvantage. Allowing the child to be cognitively passive further compromises her learning process. Use every opportunity to involve the child in the process of choice, as well as decision-making and active thinking, or she will become passive, and highly dependent.

No matter how old your child is, if you notice that she tends to be passive and allows you to make decisions for her, begin now to involve her in the thinking process. Start simple – instead of making all of the child's decisions, allow her to make choices whenever there is an opportunity to do so. However, it would be best to limit the choices that you provide or she may become confused, and you will be back to seeing the child's blank facial expression.

BASIC THINKING SKILLS

There are skills that can be developed even in young children in order to improve their visual processing and thinking skills, which include the ability to:

- categorize (group like or related information together);

- compare and contrast (how are things different, and how are they alike);

- observe (watch carefully, study);

- identify patterns (a sequence in which things occur);

- look for cause and effect (does something specific happen as a result of a particular act or activity?);

- generalize (apply what is learned to a new or different situation);

- problem solve (determine appropriate method to overcome a difficulty).

Basic skill development

These basic thinking skills can be fostered through everyday activities. However, an adult needs to facilitate the learning process with the NLD child, and make the connections that the child may not make on her own.

A classic example of teaching a skill, where generalizing the learned information comes very slowly, is crossing the street and/or watching for cars. You teach the child over and over and over again that she is not to cross the road in front of traffic. This seems to be an almost universal problem with NLD kids. If you teach the youngster about traffic lights – what the red and green lights mean (stop and go for cars) and the walk light (which means that people can cross the street) – she may learn this routine fairly readily, especially if you constantly point out the rules whether you're walking or in a car. Unfortunately, there are many, many situations where there aren't lights. These youngsters continually dart out in front of oncoming traffic, and it may take many years for the child to learn to stop, look, and listen before crossing a street, when the 'cue' of a traffic light isn't present. The child will not generalize the learning to a situation where there are no lights. She does not understand that the light takes the place of thought, and if there isn't a light, there is a series of connections that you must make on your own. Therefore, it can be quite dangerous for the child when crossing streets where there is no intersection with traffic lights, or worse yet, when she is in parking lots.

Parking lots are even more difficult for these youngsters to navigate. The visual field is very cluttered (lots of cars and people), she has to watch for cars moving down the aisles or backing out of parking spaces, there are sounds coming from many directions, and there is danger in walking between parked cars because someone might open a door and hurt her. It's imperative that you teach the child that she is not to move unless you are holding her hand. Maybe the embarrassment of having her hand held as she gets older will help her to remember the rules.

Thinking, making connections, and generalizing information to a new or different situation are skills which must be specifically taught to the child. The following are some ideas that you may find helpful. At the end of each suggestion, in parentheses, are the skill sets that are reinforced by the activity.

○ Go for a walk with your child. Point out things and talk to her about what you see. Point out the clouds, and note the differences between the big puffy clouds and the thin wispy clouds. Note dark clouds, and talk about what that represents – when the clouds get big and puffy and very dark, it might rain – that's how the sky looks when it rains. If the clouds are big, puffy, and dark, and it's very cold, then it might mean snow. Rain comes when it is warm outside, and snow comes when it is cold – it's frozen rain. Make connections for her. (*Observe, patterns, compare and contrast, cause and effect.*)

- Talk about the seasons, especially if you live in an area where the four seasons are distinct. Explain to the child what happens during each season, and when the seasons change, point out what is happening – the leaves are changing color, what does that mean? They are going to fall off, and soon it will be cold and may snow. To the NLD child, the environment is probably a mystery, so you must make sense of it for her. (*Observe, patterns.*)

- Point out the implications of a certain situation. As you are walking after a rainstorm, show the child that you are walking on firm ground. Show her the muddy areas that aren't good to walk on. Explain what happens – you will get lots of mud on your shoes, and it is very slippery, you could fall and get hurt, and you'll be all muddy. The child probably won't make these connections on her own. That doesn't mean that she isn't smart, it just means that her brain doesn't function by automatically making connections, so you need to train her brain to look for connections. (*Observe, cause and effect.*)

- During one of your walks, if the child sees a big toad or turtle which she wants to take home, humor her. Let her take it home, and then discuss all of the details related to keeping it as a pet. Where will it live? What would we keep it in? What would we feed it? Even if you know all of the answers, talk it through until the child can answer the questions. Help her look the information up in a book, introducing her to research skills. If you're using an encyclopedia, explain what it is, and what it's used for. If you decide to keep a toad, for instance, and you have to get it crickets for food, work with the child to figure out where to get them. Yes, she can catch crickets outside, but that might be a lot of work. Tell her that crickets can be purchased at pet-supply stores. Pull out the telephone book, and show the child how to look up pet-supply stores. Once you have located one, take the child with you to get the crickets as well as any other supplies that you might need. You're engaging her in the critical thinking process, but to the child, it's just plain fun! (*Observe, problem solve*)

If you consider a pet in the future, have the youngster think back to the toad experience. What did you have to consider? Walk her through all of the steps again. Use books. Use the computer. What kind of pet? What are their needs? Where do we get the pet, and the supplies? What do we do with it when it comes home? You're making the connections – helping the child to generalize learned information. (*Observe, problem solve, generalize.*)

∘ Watch educational television programs about things that interest her, from insects, to dinosaurs, to tornadoes or volcanoes. Talk to her about the program. Engage her. What would it have been like to live when dinosaurs roamed the earth? What would have been good and bad about that period of time? What would you do if there was a tornado coming? Prod her, encourage her to think! (*Observe, compare and contrast, problem solve.*)

∘ If the child is adept on a computer, buy software games that have a problem solving component rather than just action games. For example, the objective of the game might be, how do I get these guys from point 'x' to point 'y.' There are dozens of developmental software programs that are great fun for kids, but teach while they entertain. Software packaging should indicate an age level on the box. These ages are based on a child's developmental level. You might want to buy software that is designed for a younger child, especially if she frustrates easily. Also, be careful of programs that are too visually overwhelming. The idea is to improve her visual processing, and a complex visual field may frustrate her too much to develop this skill. (*Observe, and other skills depending on the specific application.*)

○ Computer games and other electronic games are also very good for improving hand–eye coordination, finger dexterity and concentration. Many parents are concerned that their children spend too much time on a computer. However, for the NLD child, a computer will probably be her best friend. The key is to buy programs that are appropriate, and target a specific skill (or set of skills), that you want to develop. The better software programs indicate on the packaging what skills their application targets. (*Observe, and other skills depending on the specific application.*) *Tip*: If you find that your child gets over-stimulated while playing on a computer for an extended period of time, use a timer. When it goes off, it's time to stop. Or, if your child needs forewarning, set the timer, and when it goes off, tell her that she will have ten more minutes, and set it again. When it goes off the second time, it's time to turn the computer off.

○ Most kids love hand-held electronic games. These are wonderful for when the child will be going for a long ride in the car, train, or plane. However, instead of buying games that are blood and gore, select Tetris or similar games that require thinking and strategizing. The noise can annoy other passengers, so you may require that the child play either without volume, or with earphones. If you make 'no noise' a rule from the beginning, the child will probably comply in order to be able to play. (*Observe, patterns, cause and effect, problem solve, and other skills depending on the specific game.*)

○ Board games are notoriously difficult for these children. They have significant difficulty understanding the rules, as well as the social component – turn-taking, losing gracefully and so on. Although board games are very beneficial for teaching thinking skills, you may have to wait until the child is eight or so before beginning even the simplest game. When you first introduce board games, it might be helpful to start with word games, since that may be the NLD child's strength. (*Observe, problem solve and other skills depending on the game.*)

○ Rubik's cubes and similar puzzles are excellent for teaching problem solving. However, these are also quite difficult for most NLD kids. Some will love them, and play for hours on end, trying to figure out how to move all the parts around to get them in the pattern they should be in. Others will throw them across the room and have a tantrum, finding them too difficult. Use your judgment here. Although it is a difficult skill, don't automatically assume that the child can't do this type of activity. Wait until you think that it might be a possibility, and try it. If it totally frustrates the child, then put it away. (*Observe, patterns, problem solve.*)

○ Most NLD children have an ongoing love affair with words. Encourage books, as well as sets which have both an audiocassette and book. Again, select books that teach something – whether it's about a concrete topic such as rocks, or something more abstract like friendship. The use of an audiocassette and accompanying book are excellent tools for the NLD child who has early reading difficulties. Since the audiocassette cues the child when to turn a page, she can follow along with the story, and the exercise may reinforce reading skills. Whether it does or not, the child will feel like she is reading independently. (*The skills will depend on the topic selected.*)

MORE ADVANCED THINKING SKILLS

Since the long-term goal is for the NLD child to develop more sophisticated thinking skills, it is important to continue to introduce age-appropriate activities which will expand her ability, such as higher-level analysis.

An additional aspect of thinking skills should be introduced as soon as the child seems ready, and that is the concept of identifying fact (reality, evidence) versus opinion (thought without actual proof). This is especially important since the NLD youngster often responds to everything that she hears as fact. You could say that this is true of all children, and you would be correct. However, without significant intervention, you may find that your adult child does not understand this distinction. An example here might be helpful.

A young man chooses to live in a particular part of the country specifically because, when he turns on the television each morning, the news anchor says it is the best place to live in the United States. This example may seem like a bit of a stretch, but it really isn't. Look at it from the young man's perspective. The news anchor reports information such as the weather, a local fire, a serious automobile accident, a building collapse – all of these are *facts!* The recognition that the news anchor's statement – 'It is the best place to live' – is an opinion is lost on this young man, who therefore sounds incredibly naive. This inability to distinguish fact from opinion affects NLD individuals in a variety of ways, from doing a research project for school to being a target for salespeople whose 'pitch' includes statements such as 'this is the best vacuum cleaner ever made.' Therefore, it is critical to begin teaching the concept of fact versus opinion as early as it is possible for the child to understand it.

More advanced skill development

The following are additional thoughts for older children to develop further their thinking skills, including the ability to analyze and distinguish fact from opinion. As above, at the end of each suggestion, the skill sets that are reinforced by the activity are indicated in parentheses.

○ As your child gets older, continue reading books to her,
and discuss them as you go along. Talk to her about the
characters – what they are like, how old they seem to be,
what they might be feeling. Why did the author include
this chapter? What is the author trying to tell us? What
would it be like to live during that period? What do you
think the clothes were like? What food do you think they
ate? Help your child to 'read between the lines,' something
with which these children have tremendous difficulty.
When you are done with the book, discuss what the main
idea was. What were the important parts of the book? Was
there a message that the author was trying to get across,
but didn't specifically state? These are all critical thinking
skills that the child will need by the time that she is in
upper elementary or middle school. The more that you
work with her at home before she is required to use this
skill in school, the better her chances of success. (*Observe,
analyze.*)

○ Watch television commercials with your child, and once
they are over, discuss them. Explain that the purpose was
to sell a product. Ask her what the actor or character said
or did that made her want to buy the product. Ask her
how she can tell if it is true. If it is a toy that looks very
appealing and quite large on the television screen, the next
time that you are at the toy store, show her the advertised
toy. Ask her if it looks like it did on television. Is it larger
or smaller? (*Observe, compare and contrast, fact vs. opinion.*)

○ While driving in the car, if you observe an automobile
accident, point it out to your child and discuss it with her.
Did it look serious? What does she think might have
caused the accident? Does she think that the weather
conditions might have had any effect? What is the likely
impact of the accident on traffic? (*Observe, cause and effect,
analyze.*)

○ Have your child help you assemble something, such as a piece of furniture that comes in pieces, especially if it is for her use. Go over the directions together, and lay everything out on the floor in an orderly fashion, grouping items such as bolt sizes. Discuss what additional items you will need, such as tools, and have the child get them. When assembling the item, make sure that you go through each step as it is outlined in the instructions, reading the step before beginning each task. Point out whether a screw requires a Phillips head or regular screwdriver. Discuss what size hammer might be best for finishing nails. Have the child help by holding pieces together, lining up predrilled holes and so on. (*Observe, categorize, problem solve.*)

○ Involve the child in gardening activities. Discuss the location of the garden, and explain that certain plants like certain conditions, such as a particular amount of sun, a type of soil, a level of moisture, and so forth. Look at plants in a book, and have the child select plants that she likes. Help her determine if the particular plant's requirements are compatible with the location where it is to be planted. Once you have both selected plants that you like, and believe are appropriate for the location, determine what additional supplies you will need (shovel, fertilizer, and so on), and take a trip to the nursery. Review the available stock with the child, and decide how many plants you will need based on the size of your selections and the area of the garden. Once you have all of your purchases, it is time to return home and lay out the garden. Together, decide where each plant should go. Rearrange the plants in various ways to see how they might look in different positions. Discuss which plants are taller and would look best in the back of the garden. Have the child dig the holes and prepare them as needed (water, fertilizer), and then insert the plant, returning soil to hold it firmly in place. Once the garden is fully planted, allow the child to tend it (weeding, watering, and insecticide), either alone or with your assistance. (*Observe, compare and contrast, categorize, cause and effect, patterns, analyze.*)

- ○ If the child wants something new, say a bicycle, involve her in the purchase process. Tell her that you are setting a budget of 'x' dollars. Explain that different bicycles have different features and levels of quality. Work with the child to determine what all of the available features are, and then prioritize them based on her interest in each. Go to several bike shops and talk with sales personnel about the pros and cons of each make, model, and feature. Make notes at each store, and indicate the price being charged. Once all of the information has been obtained, sit down with the child and discuss it. It may be helpful to convert the information to a graphic organizer (a chart or simple visual representation of the information). Discuss with the child the advantages and disadvantages of each option, and let her decide which purchase she wants to make that is within the established budget. Once the decision is made as to what you are going to buy, and where, take the child with you when you make the actual purchase. This is an excellent exercise for older children, but be careful not to overwhelm them with information. It is the process that you are teaching, so limit the information to what she is able to manage. (*Observe, categorize, compare and contrast, patterns, problem solve, analyze.*)

The point of all of these exercises is that you want to use every opportunity as a learning experience, without the child feeling like it's work. The process will take time and thought on your part, but it is well worth it. Every time we learn something new, additional neural pathways are formed in the brain. So the more you teach your child to think, the more connections she makes and the more efficient her brain will become. This intervention is absolutely critical for your NLD child, and parents can be incredibly effective teachers. Anything and everything can be a learning experience... and should be!

SUMMARY

NLD children have weak or limited critical thinking skills. Her deficits in processing nonverbal information are a significant handicap in developing higher-order thinking skills. If the child is not engaged in active learning, she will not reach her full potential. Intervention can significantly improve the child's thinking skills.

Basic thinking skills include the ability to categorize, compare and contrast, observe, identify patterns, understand cause and effect relationships, generalize, and problem solve. These skills can be taught to the NLD child through everyday activities which are facilitated by an adult. The adult must point out connections that the child will not make on her own.

More advanced thinking skills include the ability to analyze information and identify fact versus opinion. Opportunities to develop these skills must also be facilitated by an adult, but can be taught through everyday activities as well.

Strategies to improve thinking skills include providing the child with choices, pointing out common environmental manifestations and determining patterns or cause and effect implications. Watching television or looking at advertisements is an effective approach to teaching the difference between information sharing and selling. Computer and other electronic games with a teaching component are an exceptional method of learning for these children, and have the added benefit of improving hand–eye coordination and finger dexterity.

Spending time with the child, either reading and analyzing a book, gardening, making an important purchase such as a bicycle or assembling simple furniture are all excellent ways to develop important thinking skills in the older child.

Chapter 10

Communication Skills

NLD children invariably have a rather sophisticated vocabulary, even before entering school. This leads us to the erroneous conclusion that their communication skills are on a par with their vocabulary, or at least with that of their peer group. Unfortunately, this is not the case. As you've no doubt heard repeatedly, verbal communication represents only 35 percent or less of all human communication. Therefore, these youngsters may be missing at least 65 percent of the message in all social interaction. That's a huge disadvantage!

NLD children are unable to integrate spoken language with body language, facial expression and tone of voice in order to correctly identify the message being communicated. The NLD child will probably respond only to what she hears, resulting in constant misunderstandings.

Nonverbal communication is the first 'language' that neurologically typical babies learn. They quickly develop the ability to process facial expression and tone of voice long before words have much, or any, meaning. Somewhat later they integrate body language into the message. All or most of these skills precede the child's ability to communicate verbally. NLD youngsters are unable to process the individual components of nonverbal communication, and are therefore unable to integrate them into a meaningful message. If a five-year-old child falls down, the parent may say, 'You are such a klutz.' The child listens to the words, but also hears a loving tone of voice, and sees the smile on her parent's face. She knows that the parent is sending a message of love and support. The NLD child, who is exclusively dependent on words, perceives the message as negative, and may get quite upset, feeling unloved and alone with her hurt.

Often these youngsters are perceived as having odd behavior or being uncooperative. What is actually happening is that they are seriously handicapped in their interaction with others, missing more than half of the intended message. They often misunderstand what is said because there are blanks in the script that most children can fill in on their own. If you tell a child that there is no climbing on chairs, you may mean that there is no climbing on furniture. So, if the child promptly gets off the chair and climbs up on the table, you become angry, assuming that she is just being fresh. Not so. She heard what you said, and responded to the words, having no idea that you meant something else. There were blanks in what you said – your intent.

In order to get the whole message, the child must be able to process and integrate what isn't being articulated. The following skills are necessary for people to be good communicators:

- ○ the ability to 'read' body language;

- ○ the ability to interpret facial expressions;

- ○ the ability to process tone of voice;

- ○ the ability to integrate the spoken word with body language, facial expression, and tone of voice;

- ○ the ability to intuit what the other person means, but does not specifically say;

○ the ability to understand multiple meanings of words, and match the correct meaning with the word which is being used;

○ the ability to understand whether or not someone is speaking directly to you, rather than to a group of individuals;

○ the ability to understand deceit, sarcasm, metaphors, exaggeration, and similar messages;

○ the ability to initiate, maintain, and close a conversation, including listening and probing skills.

These are all nonverbal skills, areas of deficit for NLD youngsters. By simply reviewing the list, it should be obvious that these children would have significant difficulty interacting with others. Adults tend to be very concrete and direct in their communication with very young children, so the miscommunications may not be obvious. However, by the age of five or six, nonverbal skills are expected to be developing, and communication becomes less concrete. For the NLD child, this is when her communication difficulties should become quite evident. Although she has a well-developed vocabulary, the child is often confused, continually misunderstanding what is said to her and, as a result, appears easily frustrated.

Let's take a closer look at the components of nonverbal communication so that we can better appreciate the significance of each of these deficit areas for NLD children.

COMPONENTS OF NONVERBAL COMMUNICATION
Body language

We send many messages through our body language. When someone is standing in front of us with their fists resting on their hips, we immediately register annoyance. If they are standing with their arms crossed, tapping their foot, we also 'see' annoyance. If someone is sitting with their hands resting in their lap, their legs extending in front of them, and crossed at the ankle, we understand that they are relaxed and 'open.' If an individual is sitting in a chair, leaning forward, they appear to be interested and listening intently. Understanding these signals is crucial to effective communication, and the ability to process the entire message that is being conveyed.

Facial expression

Even more than we use our bodies, we use facial expressions to convey a myriad of signals. A cocked brow may mean, 'Oh, really?' A smile means we are happy. A frown may mean sad or angry. Pursed lips send a message of annoyance. Rolling your eyes may mean that you don't believe what someone is saying, or you think that they are an idiot. A relaxed face may mean that someone is lost in thought, or listening intently. Eyes wide open may mean fear or surprise. It is easy to see how a facial expression may 'control' the verbal message, either by reinforcing what is being said, or contradicting the spoken word. Or, the facial expression may *be* the message. Without the ability to integrate the facial and spoken message, communication breaks down.

Tone of voice

Tone of voice can dramatically alter the intent of the spoken message. A sharp tone of voice communicates annoyance or anger. A high-pitched voice may represent fear or excitement. A loud voice may mean anger or excitement. A soft-spoken message may be telling us that we should keep our voices down. A message conveyed in a whisper may mean that it is a secret, or that there is no talking allowed. The same verbal communication can have multiple meanings, depending on the individual's tone of voice.

Intuit or read between the lines

When we communicate with others, we often use a shorthand of sorts, not always conveying a complete message, assuming that the other individual will be able to understand what we are saying. Let's look at a simple example of how this happens.

Two youngsters go to a movie together. Upon leaving the theater, one says to the other, 'Well, what do you think?' The NLD child doesn't understand the message and may draw a total blank, or may be thinking, 'What do I think of WHAT?' The implied message from the first youngster was, what did you think of the movie? There are two nonverbal cues at play here: the word 'think' should be construed to mean opinion, and the solicited opinion was about the movie that they had just seen, although not specifically stated. The NLD child who is aware of her difficulties is stuck – if she asks for additional information, she may be perceived as a complete dunce, and if she doesn't, she can't answer the question, and may be perceived as a dunce anyway.

Multiple meanings

Unfortunately, we often have multiple meanings for words that are pronounced and spelled identically. The neurologically typical child will learn to use the context of a sentence or message in order to determine the particular usage of a word. The NLD child often interprets the most obvious meaning of a word, and misses the intended meaning. This misunderstanding of intent is likely to happen more frequently in conversations than while reading. Conversations require faster processing than does reading, where the NLD youngster is better able to use the context of a story to understand the meaning of a word. In a conversation, there is an expectation of rapid processing which the NLD child doesn't have. An illustration of a simple word which conveys several very different meanings is the word 'run.' When the word is used in the sentence 'Let's go for a run' it should be taken literally: we are going to run somewhere. When the same word is used as follows – 'I need to run this computer program' – the meaning becomes unclear to the NLD child. And if Mom says, 'I'm going to run some errands,' the child may wonder why her Mom isn't going to take the car to do her errands.

When we hear children say 'Huh?' we assume that they weren't listening carefully. However, with NLD children, it is more likely that she was listening just fine, but your message was unclear, leaving her confused. A response of 'you heard what I said' will only make the child more anxious, because it was the meaning that baffled her, and she doesn't understand why you are annoyed with her.

Intended recipient of message

If we are one of a group, and an individual speaks to us, even if our name is not used to single us out, we know if the message is intended for us individually, or is directed to the group as a whole. We look for nonverbal cues such as whether or not the speaker makes direct eye contact, or points to us as they speak. If the individual is addressing the group as a whole, they might visually scan the group, or move from individual to individual communicating through eye contact while they speak. Individuals with NLD may miss these cues, and are unable to determine whether they are being spoken directly to or not. In most cases, the NLD youngster will assume that the speaker is addressing her specifically, and will respond accordingly. Rather than being perceived as polite, the child may be considered rude for blurting out a response.

You may first notice this difficulty of understanding whether a message is directed specifically at the child when they view television programmes. Very young NLD children often believe that actors on a television show are 'real people' talking directly to them. The NLD child doesn't understand that there is an audience of millions of people throughout the world sitting in front of their televisions, nor does she understand that Sesame Street isn't a real street, but a studio. This apparent inability to separate fiction from reality creates many difficulties for NLD children. Although this is probably common with all young children, it takes much longer for the NLD child to have the correct perception.

Understanding the hidden message

The NLD youngster has significant difficulty in determining the hidden message in a conversation. They are concrete in their interpretations and will probably miss deceit or sarcasm which is directed at them. They will also fail to recognize the meaning of metaphors, idioms, exaggerations, and other more subtle forms of communication. Although metaphors and idioms may be puzzling, and limit their conversational effectiveness, deceit, sarcasm and exaggerations can actually cause very serious problems.

Picture the ten-year-old NLD child whose friend, angry with his parents for whatever reason, confides that his parents are mean, don't love him, beat him, and confine him to his room. The neurologically typical child would consider all of the facts – that she knows the parents quite well, they seem kind and loving, and she also knows that her friend tends to exaggerate. If there is any question of truth in the child's mind, she will talk it over with her parents. However, the NLD child, taking these statements at face value and worrying about her friend, has been told at school to tell the school nurse if she ever hears of this type of situation. Therefore, doing what she feels is right, she tells the school nurse, who is then required to report suspected parental abuse to the state authorities. The poor NLD child likely gets in trouble with her parents, and is completely confused as to why – after all, she did what she was told to do.

Worse yet, think of the young NLD adolescent girl, lured by an older boy who 'wants to be her friend.' The young girl, craving friends and acceptance, is an easy target for predators, with potentially disastrous results.

Theory of mind

Another area of difficulty which further compromises communication for NLD youngsters is their inability to understand another person's perspective. This is sometimes referred to as 'theory of mind.' Basically, it means that the NLD child is unaware that other people have separate and different beliefs, emotions, attitudes, or knowledge. The NLD youngster does not understand that other people think and respond differently than she does – she is unable to put herself in another's shoes. This often leads to misunderstandings, where the NLD child is chided for being insensitive or self-centered.

Let's consider what happens when two young girls have a disagreement. The NLD child becomes very angry and says mean things to her friend, and the friend begins to cry. An adult steps in and tells the NLD child that she should apologize, which she does. The other child continues to cry. The NLD child then says, 'What's your problem? I apologized, didn't I?' She doesn't understand that her friend's feelings are hurt, and although the apology was appropriate, it didn't immediately 'fix' the problem. The child, whose feelings are hurt, can't turn off the tears like turning off a faucet. She is likely to be reprimanded again for being fresh, and again she doesn't understand what she did that was wrong.

Conversational skills

Good conversational skills require that an individual is able to initiate a conversation, effectively maintain it, and appropriately close the conversation. In order to do so, she needs to be able to listen well, and probe for additional information. Neurologically typical children are adept at identifying the theme of a conversation, and participating by sharing their own experiences or thoughts on the theme. NLD children do not understand the 'rules of engagement.' They may not have the foggiest idea of how to initiate a conversation with one individual, let alone a group of children; they may be unaware that there is a theme to the conversation; they are apt to jump in with a totally unrelated topic and ramble along, having no clue as to how to disengage. Although the NLD child may be listening closely to the words being said, she probably hasn't the slightest idea that there are conversational rules which should be followed.

To summarize, the child understands words, but generally on a concrete level; she probably misses tone of voice, facial expression, body language, hidden messages, and deceit, and may be unable to initiate, maintain, or bring closure to a conversation. NLD children's communication skills are seriously impaired, and need significant intervention.

INTERVENTION

Now that we've outlined the magnitude of the problem, what can be done to help these children overcome, or compensate for, their many areas of communication difficulty? Actually, quite a lot! There is a tremendous amount that you, as parents, can teach her on a daily basis. However, this is an area where professional help will pay huge dividends. Speech and language pathologists (SLPs) are trained to screen, identify, assess, and treat language difficulties (including pragmatics, the functional use of language), as well as the social aspects of communication (including ineffective social skills). It is important to first pursue SLP services through your child's school. Because the NLD child has a communication handicap, she should qualify for speech and language services through the educational district at no cost. If you are unable to secure services through the school, then you might consider locating an SLP who will provide the services privately, and attempt to have the costs covered by your health insurance carrier. Depending on the particular school district, and/or insurance carrier, results to obtain SLP services vary. However, even if you are unable to arrange for the district or insurance carrier to cover the expense, the intervention *is* necessary. If you can afford to pay the costs on your own, or figure out another way to cover the expense, please do so. If not, the full responsibility for communication intervention will rest on your shoulders. This is a significant burden, and would be far easier if you were only required to supplement and reinforce what an SLP is teaching your child.

How the parent can help

Whether you are working with a speech and language specialist, or putting together your own communication intervention program, the following suggestions may be helpful in working with your NLD child.

- Point out body language wherever possible. Explain what the message is behind the body language. As the child gets older, use opportunities to point out expressions of body language, and ask the child if they can tell you what the 'silent' message is. This can actually be a fun exercise sometimes called 'people watching.' When you are at a mall, sit and watch as folks go buy and try to figure out whether they are happy, sad, angry, tired, or whatever by the way they hold their bodies. The point is to show the child that people convey messages through their bodies as well as through words.

- Interpreting facial expressions can be taught in a manner very similar to body language. For the young child, pointing out simple facial expressions is sufficient. As they master the basic happy (smile), sad (tears), angry (pronounced scowl), then begin to add the more subtle expressions of fear, anxiety, fatigue, and so on. Use the same exercise outlined above for people watching. Sitting at the mall, or some other public place, try to identify the feelings of individuals just by their facial expressions. As the child begins to master this, then combine facial expression with body language and see if she can identify the individual's mood. Another technique is to watch a television show or video without the volume, as in the days of silent films. See if the child can follow the story line without the words, and help her so that she doesn't get frustrated. The idea isn't to get the correct story line, but to identify the characters' facial expressions and the moods that they represent. We are trying to draw the child's attention toward the facial expressions of another individual. Using this same technique with television cartoon shows is quite fun, because the characters' actions tend to be exaggerated, and easier for the child to identify.

° In addition to being unable to read the facial expression of others, many NLD children have limited facial affect, meaning that they do not themselves show a full range of emotion on their faces. It is as important to teach the child that her facial expressions send a message which, if not appropriate to the situation, may turn other people off. Once she has learned to identify facial expressions of other people or characters, have her practice different expressions, preferably in front of a large mirror. Sit with her, demonstrate the facial expression, and then have her try it while looking at herself in the mirror. This will probably take a lot of practice, but she will learn, and it is incredibly important.

° An effective strategy for reinforcing body language and facial expressions, especially for the older child, is through games. Both charades and mime require exaggerated facial expression and body language – the point is to convey a message using only those two nonverbal skills. If the child is willing, encourage family members to play these games in a non-threatening manner to help the child improve recognition and projection of facial expression and body language.

○ Sound sets a mood. Generally the sound will be a person's tone of voice, but sometimes it is music instead. Teach the child that people use different tones of voice based on what they are feeling. Identify which tones go with which moods, or what the possibilities may be. Laughter isn't a tone per se, but it's easy to explain that laughter means that a person is happy about something. A loud voice may mean either anger or excitement, and the child will have to look for other cues to determine which it is. Is the person smiling or scowling? If they are smiling, then loud + smiling = happy. However, loud + scowling = angry. We've become almost immune to the role music plays in a movie. However, it sets the mood, and allows you to anticipate what is going to happen. Creepy music means that something scary is going to happen. The idea is to point out to the child the role that sounds, tone of voice and music, play in communication.

○ As with facial expressions, it is important to teach the NLD child that she also projects a message with her voice. Many NLD children speak in a monotone, place the inflection on the wrong part of a sentence, or speak with an inappropriate pitch. However, this deficit is more difficult for a parent to correct. If your child's tone of voice or inflection is significantly inappropriate, it would be wise to enlist the aid of a Speech and Language Pathologist.

○ Integrating spoken language, body language, facial expression, and tone of voice is bringing quite a bit of information together. This may be incredibly difficult for the NLD child, and will probably come later rather than sooner. Ideally, the school's SLP should be incorporating

communication skills in all aspects of the child's
curriculum. Remember that the child needs to have a fairly
solid understanding of each component part before trying
to integrate two or more sources of information. The more
opportunity that the child has to work on these skills, the
better her progress will be. However, it is likely that you
will still be developing this skill when your child finally
leaves the nest, and maybe even after that.

○ Humans are unique in their ability to understand the
hidden message in our communications with each other.
However, for individuals with NLD, it is extremely
difficult. They need to be taught cognitively how to
determine whether or not there is a hidden message, and if
so, what it is. Therefore, it is important to use figures of
speech and colloquial expressions from the time that the
child is young, explaining what they mean each time that
you use them. Rather than avoid using expressions such as
'I'm dead,' fearing that the child will not understand,
simply explain that it is a figure of speech that people use
when they mean that they are very tired. If you identify
each saying as you use it, the child will begin to identify
them when used by others, and eventually incorporate
these expressions into her own language. When this is
handled consistently, the child will probably learn rather
readily, since they do so well with words. Rather than try
and tease out the differences between similes, metaphors,
and so on, leave that to the child's teacher. For
communication purposes, it is wise to keep it simple by
bucketing everything into the category of 'figures of
speech.'

○ Sarcasm can be taught along with facial expressions. You
might explain to the child that when someone is sarcastic,
they don't mean what they say, and the intent of the words
generally doesn't match the person's facial expression. For
instance, if someone is trying to give you a compliment,

they might say 'You are just so cool,' and they would have a smile on their face. If, on the other hand, the individual is being sarcastic, they might use the words 'You are just so cool,' but they wouldn't be smiling. Because sarcasm can be very subtle, it is important to point it out to the child whenever you hear it, identifying for her the cues that indicate to you that it is sarcasm.

○ The more difficult instruction relates to deceit. Although this causes hurtful situations when the child is young, it is a significant danger to the older child, teen, and young adult. Naive NLD youngsters grow up to be naive NLD adults – perfect targets for predators. Since it is impossible to protect her from all potentially dangerous situations, it is important to teach her not to trust too readily. Sad as that may be, it is necessary for all children today, and critical for NLD youngsters. We must teach these children the 'street smarts' which seem to come more naturally to neurologically typical children. She should never be encouraged to blindly respect authority, and must be taught that respect is earned, and applies to adults as well as to kids. It is important that she understand that if someone says that they want to be her friend, there may be an ulterior motive. Someone may say that they want to be her friend in order to get something from her, and that something could be extremely dangerous – in the case of a young girl, it could be rape.

○ Whenever the child expresses unease with an individual or a situation, validate her feelings. Investigate her concern, and if the fear was valid, commend her for being sensitive to danger. If the situation did not represent danger, tell her that it is wise to be cautious, and to come to you whenever she feels discomfort of any kind. Reassure the child about the situation, and keep a watch yourself. Just because the original concern may not have been valid, it doesn't mean that her discomfort was unwarranted. If she expresses feelings of anger toward a teacher, and you know that the teacher is an idiot, don't give her the 'you must respect your teachers' lecture. Instead, talk through the problem, and how best she can handle it. 'I don't like Mrs. P,' may mean your child doesn't comprehend what Mrs. P is saying. If the situation is beyond her, it might be best to step in and have the child changed to another teacher. She needs to know that when she communicates her feelings, you will be there for her. Self-advocacy is an important skill for these children, and it starts with them expressing their problems to you, their parent, and knowing that they will be listened to.

○ Related to the problem of recognizing deceit is the NLD youngster's problem with taking another's perspective, or the concept of theory of mind. She may not understand that other people have different interests, and that if she invites a friend to come to her home, the friend might not enjoy the snakes that the NLD child has as pets, and may run for home when a slithering creature is thrust at her. Before a friend is to come to the child's home, the parent should sit down with the NLD youngster and explain the possible pitfalls. It would be very beneficial to discuss what another child may find fun or frightening. This should continue until the child can articulate to the parent what should be considered when a friend is coming to visit.

○ In addition, the NLD child may not realize that she should consider the effect of her words on another individual. She is apt to blurt out at a very inappropriate time, 'Mommy, she's fat!' or 'Mommy, he's ugly!' The child needs to learn that although something may be true, it may also be hurtful.

○ NLD children are very concrete; they think in terms of black and white, have a strong sense of right and wrong, and are refreshingly honest. However, there are times when total honesty is not socially appropriate. Therefore, although it might sound strange, we actually need to teach these children how to lie. Yes, lie – because it is a part of human communication, and sometimes necessary in order to be accepted by others. We're not talking about major deceit, but the little 'white' lies that protect people's feelings. If someone asks, 'Do you like my new haircut?' they don't want to hear 'No, it looks awful!' even if that is the truth. Explain to the NLD child that the truth can sometimes be hurtful, and that people who say hurtful things don't make friends (or whatever seems appropriate in your particular situation). Practice scripting those age-appropriate situations where it would be more socially acceptable to tell a little 'white' lie, rather than the honest truth.

○ Often NLD children assume that you know what they are thinking. This can be very confusing to the child who may be feeling sick at school, and expect that you will come to take her home, without first having to call and tell you. It isn't that they think you're clairvoyant, they just assume that you think the same thing that they do. Therefore, the child must be taught that other people, you included, don't know what she is thinking. You need to explain to her that what she is thinking is a secret until she tells someone.

THE CONSEQUENCES OF MISCOMMUNICATION

The child's significant communication difficulties often result in what might appear to be an old-fashioned temper tantrum. However, this is no willful child, reacting negatively to not getting her own way. She is a child with a serious disability who becomes unglued when she can no longer cope. Let's look at what might cause an after school 'tantrum.'

Each day the child goes off to school only to be confused by much of what the teacher says, by the unwritten rules of conduct, by conversations that she doesn't understand, by lunch and recess that are a nightmare – there are no friends to ease her pain and struggle. At the end of each day, after the final insult of being bullied and teased on the bus ride home, she is greeted by her mother with 'How was your day dear?' The child's frustrations of the day immediately boil over, and she lashes out at her Mom. She feels totally alone and frightened. If her mother really loved her, she wouldn't send her off to that horrible school every day to suffer again and again. The child's anger escalates and she starts screaming and slamming around the house, shouting at her Mom that she hates her, and that she wants to be dead! These explosions are 'fondly' referred to as meltdowns, and may sound all too familiar. The child is clearly overwhelmed by a day fraught with misunderstandings and perceived slights, and it comes pouring out of her.

Making sense out of chaos

So, what to do? First, understand that this is not a temper tantrum in the traditional sense. Take a deep breath. Do not get sucked into your child's venting, and don't try to stop it too abruptly. Although there should be acceptable limits – no hitting or causing damage – allow her to vent in order to get the anger and frustration out of her system. Once she begins to calm down, walk through the events of her day, eliciting what incidents took place to upset her so. Since she will face constant personal challenges, anger and frustration will be an unwelcome but common companion. It is important for her to know what is causing her anger and frustration, because it is quite likely that she won't make the connection on her own. Where there is a solution that is realistic for her to handle on her own, provide it to the child, as well as how best to anticipate the problem next time. If the problem is not something that you should expect her to deal with on her own, handle it yourself. Try not to focus on only the negative events – elicit the positive moments of the day as well. A simple smile from a teacher, or just the fact that there were no difficult moments are positives worth noting. By using this type of approach to improve the child's communication skills, you are also modeling problem solving skills, and drawing her attention to both the positive and negative events provides a balanced perspective that she is not likely to see on her own.

It is incredibly stressful for these children to manage in an environment as overwhelming as school for an entire day. As a result, it doesn't take much to derail them. A perceived slight on the school bus in the morning can throw off her entire day. Getting to the root of the problem, and providing the child with a solution, is very important, or she may perseverate about it forever. Let her know that you are in control, even if she isn't. The NLD child desperately needs reassurance that you understand her and will help and protect her.

Be a detective

If the child is having daily or frequent meltdowns when she arrives home from school, you need to do some detective work. The more frustrated and anxious the child is during her school day, the less able she is to learn the school curriculum. You need to find out why she is continually coming home exhausted and frustrated. Remember the opening statement in Chapter 7? *'The single most important thing that you can do for your child is to provide her with the right environment.'* This applies at school even more than at home, because at least at home you are there for her, whereas at school she is alone. The next important statement presented in Chapter 7 was that *'there is a direct correlation between the child's meltdowns and either our unrealistic expectations of her, the complexity of the environment, or both.'* Constant temper tantrums or meltdowns after school could be a warning indicator that teachers and school staff are not meeting her needs. So, play Sherlock Holmes for a while and determine where things aren't working for her at school, and request the appropriate changes.

SUMMARY

Sixty-five percent or more of communication is nonverbal, consisting of body language, facial expression, tone of voice, and integrating the spoken word with all three of these nonverbal forms of communication. In addition, the NLD child needs to understand the multiple meanings of a word, whether or not she is being directly spoken to, understand what is meant but not stated, recognize deceit, sarcasm, and figures of speech. If all of that isn't enough, she must also be able to initiate, maintain, and close a conversation.

NLD children process communication very concretely, and may appear to be uncooperative, rude, or fresh. However, this is often because they do not understand what is meant, but only what is said.

These youngsters need to be specifically taught that body language, facial expressions and tone of voice each send their own message, and that these nonverbal communications may not be in sync with what someone says. They also need direct instruction in the finer points of communication, such as how to recognize dishonesty and identify figures of speech. And they need to understand that other people have their own ideas and thoughts.

Environmental stressors, particularly difficulties with communication, create high levels of frustration for NLD children, often resulting in temper tantrums or meltdowns.

If possible, enlist the aid of a speech and language pathologist as you work with your child to improve their communication skills. The following are some of the things that a parent can do with their NLD child to improve their nonverbal communication:

- ° 'people watch' or watch cartoons without sound for facial expressions and body language;

- ° practice facial expressions and body language in front of a mirror;

- ° play charades or mime for facial expressions and body language;

- ° identify inconsistencies for the child between nonverbal and verbal messages;

- ° teach that respect is earned, whether for a child or an adult;

- ° teach the child to lie, especially 'white lies' to protect other people's feelings;

- ° teach that thoughts are secrets until shared, and that other people have their own thoughts, interests, and feelings;

- ° use and teach commonly heard figures of speech.

Chapter 11

Social Skills

Communication skills and social skills are naturally intertwined; however, they have been separated into two chapters in order to peel apart all of the subsets of each. We generally think of social skills as the ability to have friendships, but it actually goes far beyond that. It is an individual's ability to interact with their cultural environment. In addition to integrating all of the verbal and nonverbal information involved in a social interaction, the child needs to know when to do what, how, and with whom. Adding to the complexity of the problem is that social demands vary depending on age, so the NLD child always seems to be playing catch-up. Just when she seems to have 'gotten it,' her peer group has already moved to the next developmental level, and adolescence is a particularly difficult time for these youngsters.

In addition to the many facets of communication skills which were covered in the previous chapter, there are additional skills required for effective social interaction, including understanding the audience, reciprocity and turn-taking, proximity, appearance, and impulse control, cooperative interaction, and perspective taking. NLD children experience varying degrees of difficulty in all of these areas.

UNDERSTANDING THE AUDIENCE

Most children learn very quickly to adjust and adapt their communication depending on who they are interacting with. Young children realize very quickly that they shouldn't use 'bathroom language' when an adult may overhear – they save these gems for sharing with their peer group. A young teen knows not to tell an 'off color' joke to the school principal, unless he wants to receive a detention. Without being conscious of the process, a neurologically typical child who is faced with a social interaction does several things: identifies and categorizes the individual (peer, older student, teacher, parent), measures what he planned to say against the anticipated reaction of the recipient, and then either avoids, alters, or proceeds with what he planned to say. For most children, this process occurs in a split-second. However, all too often, the NLD child fails to perform this 'audience check.' She may have heard a joke during recess which her classmates thought was hilarious. Craving acceptance, she decides to tell her teacher the joke, only to find that the teacher rejects the child's behavior as inappropriate. Rather than receiving the teacher's favor, the child is marched to the principal's office, totally confused as to what she has done wrong, and fearful of what is to happen next.

TURN-TAKING AND RECIPROCITY

The concept of turn-taking doesn't come naturally to children. However, parents and teachers explain to them that everyone has to wait their turn. On the playground, they line up to use a piece of equipment such as a swing, are allowed a specific amount of time to enjoy the activity, and must then relinquish it to the next child. However, the NLD child doesn't readily grasp the concept of turn-taking or time. She may not realize where the line is, and cut in front of the other children. Or, she may not get off the swing when the time has come because of her difficulty understanding how much time has elapsed. In a chaotic environment such as a playground, the child may also forget to remember the rules.

Effective social interactions require conversational give and take between parties. One speaks, the other listens – then it's the listener's turn to speak, and so on. In order to know when it's your turn to speak, you must be aware that the other person has finished speaking. Have they just paused to catch their breath or collect their thoughts, or does the pause mean they are finished talking? What was the person's tone of voice; did it seem to go up at the end, meaning they are asking a question? Is the question directed at me (if there are more than two involved in the conversation)? Knowing when to speak requires good awareness of nonverbal cues, and appropriate timing. Since the NLD child's awareness of nonverbal cues is lacking, she does not have the appropriate information to determine when to enter the conversation. Inevitably, she interrupts, talks over someone else, or mutely stands there, not responding.

PROXIMITY

There are unwritten rules governing physical proximity in social interactions. The distance between two people is dependent on the relationship of the parties. Very close proximity denotes intimacy, and excess physical space means non-involvement. Children seem to learn appropriate physical proximity almost intuitively. With their parents, they are close, sitting on their laps or cuddling. When playing with friends, neurologically typical children seem to know just the right amount of space to allow between themselves and other children. They allow still more space between themselves and authority figures such as teachers, showing respect for the adult's position. NLD children are often unaware that physical proximity is an issue, let alone that it sends a message. In addition, due to their spatial difficulties, the child may have a faulty sense of where they are in relation to other people and objects. Therefore, these children may either be right in your face, or standing back so far that they are perceived as totally uninvolved.

APPEARANCE

An individual's appearance provides valuable nonverbal inform-ation. Rightly or not, it is human nature to have initial perceptions of someone based on their clothes and how they wear them, the way they wear their hair, their jewelry and so on. A quiet, studious, middle school-age child would probably avoid another student who is dressed entirely in black, with multiple body piercings, and a prominent tattoo. Why? Because the quiet, studious child would perceive the other student as a 'tough' kid who was not interested in school work, and hung around with a 'bad' crowd. The NLD student would probably not make these mental connections between appearance and likely personality characteristics. Nor is the NLD child apt to understand that they also project an image, or what that image might be.

IMPULSE CONTROL

There are societal rules for behavior, and what is considered appropriate, based on both age and setting. One of the first things that we teach young children is impulse control. Parents rarely tolerate temper tantrums, or fresh, inappropriate behavior and teachers not at all. Children quickly learn the consequences of not controlling their baser impulses, and will stop and think before acting out. Social situations are very challenging for NLD youngsters, and may be overwhelming if they occur in a public setting. When she is overwhelmed by the situation or over-stimulated by the environment, the NLD child may have limited or no impulse control. She may become extremely silly – however, this is probably a response to stress, not a controlled behavior. Unfortunately, the NLD child is often misunderstood, and adults may perceive her behavior as intentional and attention-seeking, and respond accordingly.

PERSPECTIVE TAKING

We take for granted the ability to consider another person's perspective or, to put it another way, the ability to put ourselves in someone else's shoes. If something sad happens to a friend, we immediately consider how we would feel under the circumstances, and empathetically reach out to them. Although we may have shared interests with a friend, we are also aware of other facets of their lives, and take an interest in those things even if they don't directly relate to us. Individuals with NLD don't have this intuitive sense of taking another's perspective. The NLD child tends to think that other people think and feel the same way as she does, and can appear very insensitive and selfish, although that is not her intent.

COOPERATIVE INTERACTION

Cooperative interaction is at the heart of any effective inter-personal contact. Individuals with good people skills take an interest in the other individual, understand their point of view, comfortably problem solve any conflict, and understand that both, or all, involved parties need to feel valued and treated fairly. NLD individuals don't naturally recognize that the other individual may have different interests or a different point of view, do not have fluid problem solving skills (especially when a situation is emotionally charged with conflict), don't understand the social rules of fair play, and generally fail in their attempts at cooperative interaction. This difficulty is apparent in the play skills of young children, as well as in academic team activities at school for NLD students of all ages. It is generally in the area of cooperative interaction that we see the most pronounced deficits of the NLD child.

The end result of the significant communication deficits covered in the previous chapter, and the additional social deficits outlined above, is that the NLD child is largely misunderstood by adults, and either avoided, teased, or bullied by her peer group. This is a cruel fate for any child, but for the sensitive NLD youngster who is probably knocking herself out to do the 'right' thing (if only she knew what that was), the long-term implications can have disastrous results. These children have average, to above-average intelligence, are aware that they are somehow different, and want desperately to fit in, be accepted, and have friends. When the adults in the child's life also fail her, it is no wonder that we see such a high level of anxiety and depression in such a young population.

As in all other areas of the child's life, we must teach her the skills required to be socially accepted and have friends. It is time-consuming and hard work, but she can be taught appropriate social skills. Although she may never be as spontaneous as she'd like, with the right kind of intervention, she can learn what she needs to in order to have friends and be a well-accepted member of society. Much of her success will depend on how willing both of you are to invest the time and effort.

STRUCTURED PLAY

Most NLD children will require structured play. Whether she is four or 14, she will probably need ongoing guidance with the 'rules of engagement' when interacting with friends. The most successful situation will probably involve just two children, since a one-on-one interaction is much easier for the NLD youngster to manage than a group situation.

Before the friend comes to the house, discuss with your child what the friend is interested in. Ask about the friend's parents and whether or not there are siblings. Do they have any pets? Do they have any hobbies? The NLD child won't necessarily know the answers to these questions. However, you need to explain that it is important to know something about a friend in order to be able to understand them. This is the first stage in introducing the child to understanding the perspective of another individual. Explain to your child that if she doesn't show an interest in what her friend might want to do, he may not want to come back to play again.

Before the friend comes to your home, it is wise to sit down with your child and explain the dos and don'ts. This should be done each time a friend comes to visit until she is doing it on her own. However, she may need reminders, or a cue, for some time. A list of dos and don'ts such as the following might be helpful:

- do welcome the friend at the door;
- do take their coat and hang it up for them;
- do offer them a drink or snack if you get one for yourself;
- do ask them what they want to do because they are the guest;
- don't go off by yourself to be alone;
- don't put your headphones on while the friend is visiting;
- don't call another friend until the visiting friend has gone home.

Well, you get the idea. Depending on the age of the child, you can develop an appropriate list of dos and don'ts and go over them with the child. Explain what each item means, and why it is important. For the younger child, plan the time prior to the visit – what activities the children will do, for how long, and so on. Supervise the play so that you can facilitate the interaction and ensure a successful outcome, and keep the visit short. After the friend has left, discuss with your child how the visit went. Did she enjoy it? Did anything happen that should be discussed? Praise her for all of the things she did right. Make a mental note of the child's social mistakes, and orchestrate the next friend visit to avoid the same mistakes.

It is recommended that the social interactions between your child and her friends occur at your home, unless the other parent has a good understanding of your child's difficulties, and how best to support her. Otherwise, the social rule of 'returning the invitation' might not be a good idea.

When the child is young, you have a lot of control over who she plays with and where she goes. Make sure that her friends are positive role models, and that she is in social situations that she can manage, or has the appropriate support available.

THE PARENT AS FACILITATOR

As the child gets older, your presence shouldn't appear as intrusive. However, it is wise to continue to provide a structure for the time her friend will visit. Remember to continue the practice of discussing the interests of the friend, prodding your child to consider what might be activities that both youngsters will enjoy. Does her friend like to 'hang out' and listen to music? Or is she interested in more hands-on activities such as computer or electronic games? Naturally, the activities should be age-appropriate, but agree on options that your child won't struggle with.

If she and her friend want to play electronic or computer games, provide a timer, and explain that it should be set for the duration that each will play. This will provide the social cue that your child needs for appropriate turn-taking. Stay within hearing range of where they are playing so that you can monitor how effectively they interact, and unobtrusively step in when necessary. If it is an activity that has caused conflict, either suggest a resolution, or another activity. If they are going to listen to music, have your child ask her friend to bring some of her own favorites, once more explaining that the other child may have different musical interests.

When the friend has left, sit down with your child and discuss the visit, again reinforcing the positives, and making mental notes of the difficulties. This structured social interaction may be required for some time. You are acting as facilitator and social coach, creating an environment where the child can succeed, and teaching the important aspects of social interaction. Naturally, with the older child, the interactions will become more complex, and your 'debriefing' sessions may be longer. Just keep in mind that you want to appear as though you're simply interested, and chatting with her. Sitting the child down at the table for a report on how she conducted herself will be counterproductive. Remember, these were supposed to be *fun* activities for her!

Naturally, your NLD child will also be in settings where there are a number of children. These environments are more challenging for her, and she may become confused or overwhelmed. If your young child is invited to a birthday party, stay with her – many parents do, so it will not appear odd. You can keep an eye on her, quietly removing her from an activity if she becomes over-stimulated, or explain the rules if she becomes confused. If the party is to last for two hours, but at an hour and a half it is obvious that your child has had enough, simply make your excuses and leave.

For the older child, this is a bit more awkward. If she has friends, and is invited to a party, the last thing that you want to do is deprive her of the event. However, if it is something that you know will be too difficult a situation for your child, and she runs the risk of embarrassing herself, it might be best to avoid the situation. Keeping friends is tough enough without setting your child up for failure. For the adolescent or young teen, a school dance may be a great experience, however, discuss with her what is a realistic duration for her to stay. Can she handle the loud music, dancing and flashing lights for the entire function? Or, would it be best if she arrived late or left early?

If she will attend a party, a sleepover for instance, then make up a list of the social do's and don'ts ahead of time. Discuss what is likely to occur – lots of food, movies, very little sleep – so that she will have some idea of what to expect. Make sure that she understands that if it becomes too much, she can call you at any time and you will come and get her. However, provide her with a graceful social exit. She can make an excuse to her friends that she isn't feeling well, and gracefully exit the situation.

CHAPERONE SOCIAL EVENTS

If your child wants to attend a teen dance at her school, then offer to chaperone the event. You don't need to smother her, but it still might be a good idea if you can keep an eye on her in such a socially complex environment. If she is becoming overwhelmed, you can quietly take her for a walk, to get a break from the noise and chaos. If she is behaving inappropriately, you can intervene before it becomes a problem, and explain to her, out of earshot of her peers, what she was doing wrong, and what might be a more acceptable behavior. Remember, the operative word is unobtrusive – you are trying to facilitate social acceptance, not ostracize the child by your overbearing presence.

THE ARM'S LENGTH RULE

The mystery of physical proximity is really rather easy to address. You explain to the child that there are 'rules' that need to be followed. How close you are physically to a person sends a message of intimacy at one end of the scale, and emotional distance at the other end. Naturally for the young child, the language needs to be simple. 'With Mommy and Daddy, it's okay to sit on our laps and cuddle, but when we have visitors, you don't sit on their laps, you sit in a separate chair.' The young child may also smother her friends, by constantly hugging and kissing them. She needs to understand that we give our friends a bit more space. Maybe you implement the 'arm's length' rule, meaning that you don't get within an arm's length of anyone other than immediate family.

SOCIAL SKILLS GROUPS

Social skills groups which are facilitated by a trained professional are wonderful programs for NLD children of all ages. You may find that there are social skills groups within your child's school, or you may find appropriate groups through your local children's hospital or a clinician who specializes in this type of work. Or, you may not have access to any of these services. Whether your child participates in a group or not, you will still play a huge role in fostering social competence in your child.

THE RULES OF ETIQUETTE

With an older NLD child, the space issue may not be specifically physical, but might surface in other areas. Let's see how this might happen. Your daughter calls her friend, who is unable to come to the phone. The friend's mother says that she will take a message and have the friend return the call in a little while. She waits five or ten minutes, and no return call, so she places a second call to her friend. This may be followed by repeat calls until either the friend's mother loses her temper, or the friend takes the call. However, the NLD child has probably annoyed both her friend and the mother with her repeated phone calls. What the NLD child doesn't understand is the 'unwritten rule' that she should wait until her friend returns the call, and that it is rude to keep pestering someone with phone calls. She is 'crowding' them, but it is figurative, not literal. The rules of etiquette need to be specifically taught to the child. Phone rules might include:

- ° no calls before 9:00am;
- ° no calls between 5:00pm and 7:00pm (the family dinner hour);

- ° no follow-up calls unless three hours have elapsed;
- ° no calls after 8:00pm;
- ° no long-distance calls without specific permission.

The phone rules, like any other, should be age and lifestyle dependent. Different parts of the country or world may have cultural requirements that vary tremendously from one place to the next. Whatever the rules, the child should be provided with them, as well as with the consequences of what will happen if she violates the rules.

Many children seem to absorb etiquette without much specific instruction. This may not be the case with the NLD child. It might be helpful to buy a children's etiquette book and use it whenever a situation arises that requires that she understand the social norm for an occasion. For instance, under what circumstances do you give a gift, and what is the appropriate way to receive a gift – especially one that you don't like? She needs to understand why it is thoughtful to bring back mementos for her friends or classmates when she is on a trip.

When selecting a book on etiquette, it would be helpful if it also covered manners. NLD children tend to believe whatever they read in a book, and in this case that can work in your favor. The child may think it is very funny to stick a straw up her nose while in a restaurant, as you sit there trying to figure out how you can either disappear or lunge across the table at her. Reading and discussing the rules governing restaurant manners before eating out may make for a much more pleasant outing for both you and your child. There are some excellent books on the market that actually present etiquette and manners in a humorous fashion for both young children and adolescents.

SOCIAL JUDGMENT

Your NLD child will need specific instruction in the social rules which apply to various relationships. What the child can say at home, or private things that are discussed at home, might not be appropriate to share with someone else. She also needs to understand the social judgment required in various relationships. A relationship with another child is quite different from the relationship with a teacher. There is an expectation that students treat teachers with respect. It wouldn't do for the adolescent NLD child to slap a teacher on the back in greeting as she has seen her friends do to each other, or for the younger child to bonk her teacher on the head. Either of these actions is likely to result in the child being disciplined. Avoid as many of these misunderstandings as possible by giving the child guidelines or explicit rules to follow when dealing with various individuals.

APPEARANCE SENDS A MESSAGE

By adolescence, the NLD child should be aware of the messages people send through their appearance. Like everything else, this will take specific instruction. Point out what other age mates wear, and the image it projects. Make sure that you are aware of any gangs or tough groups in your child's school, and note what their 'uniform' appears to be. Identify these 'uniforms' to your NLD child, and explain why she shouldn't copy their appearance. Make sure that she understands that, rightly or wrongly, her peers and teachers will judge her based on her appearance, at least initially, and then explain the concept of first impressions.

In the previous chapter we saw how 'people watching' is an effective strategy for teaching facial expressions and body language. It is also an effective approach for teaching the child what role appearance plays in sending a message. Teach the child what a socially acceptable appearance looks like, and help her select a wardrobe that won't stigmatize or isolate her.

We want our children to achieve an appropriate degree of social competence and acceptance. Social skills are discrete and isolated learned behaviors. However, social competence is the smooth, sequential application of these skills in order to establish and maintain social interaction. It will take a lot of work to help your child reach a level of competence. Use all of the resources that are available to you, and give your child every advantage. Without social competence, she won't become an independent adult.

SUMMARY

In addition to integrating the verbal and nonverbal information discussed in the previous chapter, the child then needs to know when to do what, how, and with whom. There are many additional skills required of the child before she can be socially competent.

The NLD child will need direct instruction in social skills as she does with communication skills. Whether these are taught in concert with communication skills, or separately, will depend on the child's ability and whether or not she is participating in a social skills group. A review of the specific social skills which were addressed in this chapter follows:

- *Understanding the audience* The child needs to know how and when to adjust and adapt their communication depending on who they are interacting with. Teach her how to do an 'audience check.'

- *Turn-taking and reciprocity* The younger child will need specific instruction in the rules of turn-taking while playing. The older child and adolescent will need to understand the social rules of reciprocity while conversing with another. Adult facilitation will be required in order to teach these skills.

○ *Proximity* Literal and figurative 'space' issues will need to be explained to the child. The arm's length rule is an effective strategy for teaching the child about physical proximity. Scripted, written rules will help the older child understand figurative proximity issues, such as how long to wait for a return telephone call before placing a second call.

○ *Appearance* The child needs instruction in how appearance sends a message. 'People watching' is one effective way to help the child understand this concept. Help her determine what message she wants to send to others through her own appearance.

○ *Impulse control* For the young child, situations which cause a problem with impulse control should be avoided. Facilitated interaction allows the adult to control the environment. Following social interactions, 'debrief' with the child to discuss what went well, and what went wrong. Discuss a plan for avoiding the problems in the future.

○ *Perspective taking* Incorporate in the child's preparation for each facilitated social interaction an understanding of perspective taking. Discuss the interests and personality of the friend who is to visit. Explain to the child that it is important to consider the interests of her friend during the visit, or the friend may not be interested in another visit. Together determine activities that may appeal to both children.

○ *Cooperative interaction* Good communication and social skills are all required for effective cooperative interaction. Facilitated social interaction and participation in social skills groups provide opportunities for the child to practice her learned skills in a safe environment. The adult should provide positive feedback to the NLD child, and continue to develop those skills which challenge her. Be patient – this is clearly a major difficulty for her. It will probably take significant intervention in order for her to become socially competent.

Chapter 12

Independent Living Skills

As with everything else, independent living skills need to be specifically taught to the NLD individual. She will not learn these skills through observation. Adolescence seems to be about the right developmental time to begin the process of preparing her for the future when she will live on her own. Although it's rather scary to think of our adolescent eventually living away from us, we need to be working toward a goal of self-sufficiency. It would be helpful to take some time to think through the tasks that need to be taught, and the order in which that might best occur. There are dozens of things that you will need to teach the child, but in this chapter we will focus on four specific areas:

- housekeeping
- laundry
- cooking
- shopping.

Let's take a look at each of these areas, and see how we might teach the NLD youngster these important skills. Your child will have her own individual strengths and weaknesses, and may already be doing some of these things, but we'll assume that you have not yet started working with her in these developmental areas. If you are fortunate enough to be working with an occupational therapist, they can be an invaluable resource in helping to develop independent living skills, as are class offerings at the child's school.

HOUSEKEEPING

Teaching the child good housekeeping skills is an excellent place to start, because we probably begin giving our children chores to do at least by adolescence, but ideally much younger than that. There are many things that even very young children can do or assist with.

It is always important to explain to the child that the objective is cleanliness, not the task itself. For instance, when cleaning a floor, dirt is not always visible, and may be hiding under and behind things. So, in order to accomplish the objective of cleanliness, we need to find both the obvious, as well as the hidden dirt.

Washing dishes

Teaching the NLD child to wash dishes is likely no different from teaching a young neurologically typical child. The only difference may be the age at which you start. Although automatic dishwashers may seem to be the norm in all households today, we can't assume that when she has her first apartment, or is away at college, she will have a dishwasher. Therefore, she needs to be taught how to wash dishes manually, as well as how to use a dishwashing appliance.

The first major challenge that she will be faced with in washing dishes is her spatial difficulty. Although this seems to improve as NLD youngsters get older, they may still be apt to knock things over. A crowded counter and sink with lots of breakable items may be an accident waiting to happen. Explain this to her, and show her how to organize the work area to reduce the likelihood of breakage and injury. Two specific problems need to be addressed. If she uses too much force when washing a glass, it may break, causing her to cut her hand. The second danger is putting knives in a sink full of soapy water in order to let them soak. She may grab something that she feels in the bottom of the sink, only to find that it was a sharp knife which may cause serious harm.

The safe approach to manually washing dishes is to place a small basin of soapy water in the sink, so that the child is washing one item at a time. Show her how much liquid soap to use, as well as how much water, and that each item needs to be rinsed clean after washing it. Teach her how to put the clean dishes in a drying rack, making special note that utensils should be placed with sharp edges facing down (forks, knives, and so on) in order to avoid injury.

Although a dishwashing appliance may seem easier to use, there are actually several steps involved. First the child needs to be taught where each item is to be placed within the dishwasher in order to ensure that everything gets cleaned. Then she needs to understand how much soap to use, and where it is supposed to be inserted. There are generally various settings on automatic dishwashers, depending on how dirty the dishes are and whether or not you will use a delayed wash cycle. Also, turning the dial may require pushing and turning simultaneously, which might be physically awkward. If you will be teaching your child to use an automatic dishwasher, it might be wise to mark the setting that she is to turn to so that she doesn't have to remember which one it is.

Cleaning counters

Cleaning counters is a fairly simple task that can be taught to the younger child, however, she should be tall enough to reach without having to climb on a step stool or chair in order to do so. Explain to the child that although the counters may look pretty clean, food preparation may create a bacteria problem on kitchen surfaces, most particularly the counters. So, although wiping the counters with a damp sponge may be fine for surface soil, she should also clean the counter periodically with an anti-bacterial agent. Teach the younger child to clean the counters with a sponge, and when she is older, introduce the concept of a periodic cleaning with an anti-bacterial agent.

Dusting

The objective when dusting furniture is to remove the dust, and it may be hiding under or behind things. The child should be taught to go slowly and carefully so that she doesn't knock anything over as a result of her spatial difficulties. Show her the options that are available, such as a dust rag, feather duster, and so on, and the advantages that you find to each. Explain the difference between furniture wax and the spray cleaning agents that are applied to a dust rag or duster to attract dust, making it easier to clean surfaces more thoroughly. If you use either (wax or dusting spray), explain what surfaces each is used on, and whether or not they are to be applied directly to the surface being cleaned, or to the rag or duster instead. Show her that dust will build up on her rag or duster as she is working, and that she may have to take it outside to shake off the excess dust.

Trash and garbage

If you are fortunate enough to have a garbage disposal, your child will need to learn how to use it. Remember that this can be a dangerous appliance, and she should be cautioned about the dangers. For instance, if something like an eating utensil is dropped down the disposal, what is a safe method of retrieving it in order to avoid injury? There will be things that can't be put in it, such as certain types of bones, corncobs, and so on. Develop a strategy for discarding these types of materials, as well as all garbage if you don't have a disposal. Although it might seem like an expensive solution, zip-lock bags are the most efficient method. The child can be taught how to tell if the seal is closed properly to avoid both odor and creepy crawlies.

Be sure to explain that trash is picked up on a specific schedule and what day or days that occurs. Teach her what the requirements are. Are you required to recycle? If so, teach the process. Are you required to put all trash in plastic bags? Where should the trash be placed for pick-up? Also explain what time of day the trash will be collected, and if there are restrictions on when the trash may be placed outside for collection. For instance, in some cities, you are not allowed to put your trash outside until after a specific time of day.

Cleaning agents

Many cleaning agents can be quite toxic, especially those used to clean bathrooms and kitchens, while others, particularly those with bleach in them, can permanently damage fabric. Some of the agents that will make her cleaning easier fall into one of these two categories. Rather than avoid them, explain to her the danger of each, and teach her how to note the contents when purchasing them. If the agent is toxic, explain that she should wear gloves, and only work in a well-ventilated area. When working with bleach, she should be careful to cover her clothes in order to avoid permanent white polka dots all over what she is wearing. A better solution is for her to have a set of 'cleaning clothes' that she doesn't have to worry about damaging.

Cleaning floors

Let's look at various ways to clean floors. The child needs to be taught that different tools are used depending on the type of flooring material. For carpeting, we use a vacuum, with a 'carpet' setting. For bare floors, we can use a vacuum with a 'bare floor' setting, a dust mop, or a broom. A broom may be awkward for the NLD child to manage. The motion requires crossing midline (moving arms from the right to left side of the body), and the dirt and debris may fly all over the place if the motion is too brisk. For the same reason, a dust mop may also be a difficult tool for her to use. The choice of a broom or dust mop actually requires more coordination than we might think. Not only is the physical motion awkward, but she must also pick up the dirt after it is in a nice neat pile. It may be no easy task for her to get the mess onto a dustpan, and then into the trash.

What might make the most sense is to teach her how to use a vacuum cleaner so that she can do all of the dry floor cleaning with one tool, using various attachments. Another advantage to a vacuum cleaner is that the child does not have to cross midline in order to use it. When you first introduce her to the vacuum cleaner, explain what everything is and how to use each feature. Explain where the cord is if it is retractable, show her how long it is so that she knows that she may have to plug it into various outlets if she is vacuuming a large area, and identify which might be the most appropriate outlets to use. Point out where the on/off switch is, and how to use it. Show her where the bag or catch basin is and teach her how to change the bag or empty the basin. You may not start with explaining everything at once, since it could overwhelm her. That will depend on the age and ability of your particular child. Start small, having her vacuum only one room for a while – her own bedroom would be a good choice. Gradually, expand to include other areas with the same type of flooring before moving on to other types of flooring which require different attachments or settings.

For floors such as linoleum or tile, vacuuming alone will not accomplish the cleanliness objective. Periodically, she will have to use a wet cleaning agent on these surfaces. Fortunately, the use of a wet mop requires the same body motion that the child learned for handling a vacuum cleaner. Rather than providing a cleaning agent that must be mixed with water in a pail, it would be easier to provide her with something that is already prepared, and comes in a plastic spray bottle. Remember that the child's spatial difficulties may cause her to knock over a pail, and a mop and bucket approach also requires continually wringing out the mop which can be awkward and/or difficult. It is best to avoid the risk of a disastrous spill, and the extra physical demands that are difficult for her. Show her how to spray the cleanser on small areas, and mop each area until the entire floor is done.

Cleaning appliances

You will need to teach your child how to clean various appliances, and the need to do so. If dust builds up around vented areas, the appliance may not work properly. Ovens naturally become soiled and, if not cleaned periodically, may cause a fire. Stove burners have the same risk of fire if spilled food is not cleaned away.

Teaching the child to clean appliances demands more judgment than some other housekeeping tasks, and should therefore wait until the child is a bit older. If the child has learned to use a vacuum cleaner, show her how to clean the back of the refrigerator vent in order to remove dust build-up. At the same age, if you have a microwave oven, teach the child that it needs to be cleaned out with a damp sponge or glass cleaner. As long as she is tall enough to reach, there is little risk of injury when cleaning the inside of a microwave oven.

If you have a self-cleaning conventional oven, teach her how to set it to clean itself. However, it would also be a good idea to teach the youngster how to clean an oven manually for the same reason that we teach the child how to wash dishes manually. When she goes out on her own, she may not have access to the appliances which you have in your home. Cleaning agents for ovens are highly toxic, and the same safeguards that were taught for other hazardous cleaning agents should be reinforced. While cleaning an oven, she should wear rubber gloves, and open the windows, and/or use an exhaust fan.

Stovetops also need cleaning. Teach the child what cleaning agent to use, and how to remove drip pans if necessary. Make sure that she understands that she should be careful when cleaning around the dials so that she doesn't inadvertently turn on a burner.

By the time the child is in middle school, she has learned that foods spoil, even when refrigerated or frozen. At this point, involve her in the process of cleaning out the refrigerator and freezer. Show her the 'sell by' or 'use by' freshness date on packaging, and discuss whether the food is still fresh enough to eat, or should be discarded. Explain that spills need to be cleaned in the refrigerator so that bacteria does not begin to grow, and show her how to do so. Periodically, go through the freezer, and teach her how to determine whether or not frozen foods should be kept or discarded. By going through this process, you can also take the opportunity to explain what quantities of certain items to buy when grocery shopping in order to avoid spoilage.

Cleaning bathrooms

As you begin to teach your child how to clean a bathroom properly, start with cleaning the counters if there are any. Introduce this at the same time that you teach her how to clean the counters in the kitchen. The concepts are the same. A damp sponge may be fine for most days, but periodically an anti-bacterial cleanser should be used as it is in the kitchen.

Another simple task to teach her is to clean the mirror(s) with glass cleaner. However, wait until she is tall enough to do so without climbing on the sink or using a stepladder. She may need to stand on a low stool, but make sure that it is very stable, especially if she has balance problems.

Next it would make sense to teach her how to clean the sink. If she is washing dishes, explain to her that cleaning the sink is like cleaning a big bowl, except that you use different cleanser. Show her how to use the cleaning agent, and provide her with gloves if it is toxic. Somewhat later, you can move to the bathtub/shower, explaining that she cleans it the same way that she does the sink – it's just a whole lot bigger!

Last, teach the child how to clean the outside and inside of the toilet. If you do not have animals, use a tank cleanser that keeps the toilet bowl clean by releasing a cleaning agent every time that you flush (animals who drink from the toilet would become quite ill). This will reduce the amount of toilet cleaning required. Explain to her that germs breed on toilet seats, and that it is important to use an anti-bacterial cleanser on the seat.

Beds

The NLD child can be taught to make her own bed at around six or seven years old. However, the key is to eliminate the top sheet, and use a comforter instead of a blanket or bedspread. Therefore, all the child is required to do is to neatly straighten the comforter. It is helpful to have a solid color, with straight or boxed quilting lines, so that the child can determine if the comforter is squarely on the bed. The pillow is placed neatly at the head of the bed. If she keeps stuffed animals on her bed, she can arrange them neatly as well. And voilà, she is done! Since NLD children like things orderly, you may be surprised at how receptive she is to making her own bed. It could be quite some time before she is able to make her bed with a top sheet. There's no rush, although it would be helpful if you could teach her how to use a top sheet before leaving home.

By adolescence, the NLD child should be able to change her bed sheet, if she is provided with fitted sheets. Initially, she may crawl all over the bed in order to put the sheet on, and will become frustrated if she has already put a corner or two on the mattress, only to have them pop off when she crawls across the sheet. Teach her to put the sheet on the furthest corner of the mattress first, followed by the next furthest and so on, until all four corners are secure. Putting pillows in pillowcases can be awkward. Teach her how to do it in a way that is easy for her, possibly by scrunching up the case and then working it over the pillow in the same way as you put on socks. Assuming there is no top sheet, she next places the comforter squarely on the bed, puts her pillow(s) neatly at the head of the bed, and she's done. Explain to the teenager that there is a schedule for changing bedding and why, and then be consistent in when you change the sheets. Hopefully, this will become a habit by the time she leaves home.

Changing light bulbs

It may seem silly to have a separate section here for a task as simple as changing a light bulb. However, it is something that she will be required to do quite often, and has a hidden danger. If the bulb is not compatible with the light fixture, it can cause an electrical fire. Make sure that the child understands that there are wattage limitations on all light fixtures, and that she will need to know what those are when changing a burned-out bulb. Explain to her that she should never remove a bulb which has just blown out, because it will continue to be quite hot for several minutes. Also, light bulbs should never be touching anything that is flammable, such as curtains or paper. The heat from the bulb could easily cause a fire. Halogen bulbs are especially dangerous fire hazards, and you may wish to avoid them entirely. However, explain what they are to the child and why you do not use them in your home.

Create a schedule

It is very helpful to create a cleaning schedule when you begin to teach your child housekeeping skills. As in all areas, the child will respond and remember best if there is a routine. A monthly calendar would do nicely, with the various tasks written in on specific dates. If it is your practice to vacuum the house once a week, select a day of the week (for instance Monday), and write the task on each Monday of the calendar. Enter each housekeeping task on the calendar, and keep it posted in a prominent location so that the child becomes accustomed to referring to it as she assists with more and more tasks. When she finally goes off on her own, help her develop her own housekeeping calendar, spreading the tasks throughout the week so that she does not become overwhelmed by the requirements of keeping a clean home.

LAUNDRY

There are several steps in the laundry process which the child needs to be taught. The primary steps are: sorting, washing, drying, and folding. For the most part, the best age at which to begin teaching these skills is around adolescence.

Sorting

The first thing to teach is how to sort by color and fabric. The first three sorting categories are by color – white/light, color/permanent press, and dark. The child needs to understand the risk of contracting the 'pink underwear syndrome,' where you put a red item in the same wash load as white undergarments, and wash on warm or hot. The red dye, as a result of the warm water and strong pigment, will 'bleed' onto the lighter clothing. It is important for the child to understand the purpose of sorting into three color categories. Additional sorting categories may include type of fabric, such as white/light delicates versus white/light towels and bedding – with delicates being washed on a shorter, gentler agitation cycle, and towels and bedding being washed on a longer, stronger agitation cycle, possibly using hot water. Bright cottons may have different washing requirements from permanent press garments.

Most clothing now carries washing instructions on a tag sewn into a seam of the garment. Point these out to the child, so that she knows to look for the care information. This takes the mystery out of what items can be washed with the garment, and what settings to use. At the same time that you are teaching the child to use the care information tag sewn into the garment, point out the tags which say, 'dry clean only.' All garments which require dry cleaning should be stored separately from clothing that is to be washed.

Washing

Next comes instruction in the use of the washing machine, and three settings in particular – load size, clothing type, and wash/rinse water settings. She needs to know whether the load is large or small, and how to determine which size it is. Show her where a small load comes to inside the machine, as well as how high the large load level is, so that she will know what load size setting to use. She will also need to know which clothing type setting to use – delicate, permanent press, normal, and so on. Finally, she must know which water setting to select. When you teach her these settings, use the same order every time that you do laundry. This should facilitate learning for her.

Drying

The next step is drying. As your teen becomes more proficient at doing laundry, discuss what gets dried and how. Like all of the laundry steps, determining what items should be machine dried, and what items should not, needs to be specifically taught. Many delicates, and clothing items which are 100 percent cotton, will probably do best if they are line dried, either on a rack in the house, or on a line outside. Sheets and towels, socks and jeans, dry quite efficiently in an electric dryer. She will need to be taught the various heat and time settings, and as with the washing machine, these should be taught in a specific order.

Folding

When it comes to folding clothes, most children would rather just dump the clean clothes in their drawer. Although it may be tempting to allow your child to do so, it will make finding things very difficult for her. Remember that this child may have difficulty locating an item in a visually confusing environment. Therefore, everything needs to be folded and put in its proper place.

It may seem that the obvious place to start is to teach her how to fold her own clothes. However, garments can be the most difficult items to fold. Begin by teaching her how to fold the simpler items, such as washcloths, towels and pillowcases. Provide a flat surface, such as a bed, so that she can lay the item out and fold it without having to hold it in her hands and figure out what goes where. Holding an item in 'space' will probably confuse her, and she may then become frustrated and give up. Once she becomes proficient in folding simple items, move on to clothing. Start with the items that are the easiest to fold, and move on to the more difficult garments. Have her put her own clothing away once everything is folded. She is more apt to remember where her things are if she has put them away herself. In fact, it would be beneficial to have the child put her own clothing away long before you begin to teach her how to fold.

COOKING

In the US, most schools now require that all middle school children take a class which we used to call home economics. Now it may be called any one of a number of things, but commonly it is referred to as 'life science' or something similar. Find out when this class will be taught, and if it is an elective, be sure to have your child take the course. This will save you a lot of time in teaching the necessary skills for cooking. The course will cover things such as food groups, nutrition, measurements, use of a stove and oven, and other pertinent information. It would be very helpful to get a syllabus of the class so that you know what material was covered. Once your adolescent has taken the course, you can then begin to teach food preparation skills at home.

Stove

It is best to start simple, and teach the foods that your child eats on a regular basis, so that she can begin to make basic things for herself. Since she may already be making cold sandwiches, teaching her how to make a grilled-cheese sandwich could be a good way to introduce her to the stove. Have her prepare the sandwich, and then provide her with a griddle or flat pan of some type. Show her how to treat the bread or griddle with butter or whatever you use, and put it on the griddle. Discuss with her what heat setting would be appropriate, and supervise her while she cooks the sandwich. The next time she prepares a grilled-cheese sandwich, add another ingredient, such as ham, so that she knows that modifications can be made to what she is preparing.

Microwave

If you have a microwave oven, start by teaching her how to heat a ready-made pizza, or cook popcorn. Most kids like these foods, and you can reinforce what was probably already covered in her school class – reading and following the directions on the package. Show her the settings on the microwave for heat and time. Again, supervise her at least the first time that she prepares these items. Expand her microwave repertoire as she becomes comfortable with its operation. Begin with other simple foods, such as preparing a hotdog, and gradually add more difficult items that may require more than one heating cycle.

Oven

When you begin to work with the oven, it might be best to make something that she has already made in the microwave, such as the ready-made pizza. Again, refer to the directions on the package which show cooking instructions for either microwave or oven. Teach her how to set the time and temperature. Make sure that she uses oven mitts, preferably those that extend up the arm. It is easy for her to burn herself when reaching into a hot oven. Again, once she becomes comfortable with the oven, begin to add simple types of food, gradually adding more difficult food items.

Baking should probably start with simple pre-packaged items such as cookies and cakes. The prepared cookie dough which is packaged in rolls that you simply have to cut up and place on a cookie sheet is a great way to begin baking.

When she is using either the stove or the oven, she will require more supervision than with a microwave, since there is a stronger chance of injury. So, even when you think she is getting proficient with the stove and oven, keep an eye on what she is doing.

SHOPPING

Naturally, your child has been inside of stores with you for many years. However, once you begin to teach her how to shop – whether for food or clothing – it is wise to make lists, and discuss what stores would be best for her to shop in.

Food

Many supermarkets are now mega-sized operations, and may be overwhelming for the NLD child. If there is a smaller supermarket close by, this may be the best place to take her to do the shopping.

Yes, the prices may be higher, but she is more likely to be able to buy what she needs if she isn't overwhelmed by the size and available choices. It would be best to use this store before you actually begin to teach her how to shop so that she is already somewhat familiar with the environment. And then continue to use the same store, so that she will learn the layout – where the refrigerator and freezer sections are, dry goods, bakery, and so on.

If you are quite familiar with the layout of the store yourself, you can help her prepare a shopping list that is in order by how the items are found in the store. Bouncing around the store from section to section will confuse her, and she may then become frustrated and give up. Make the process as simple and stress-free as possible.

When it is time to checkout, show her how you bag the groceries. You put the boxes and canned goods on the bottom, and the softer items and things that should not be crushed on top. The bread won't look much like a loaf, if cans are piled on top of it. Also teach her about weight distribution so that she will be able to carry the bags, and also so that they don't rip the first time that she picks them up. It would be helpful to bag the frozen and refrigerated foods separately from other items.

Be sure to explain to her that you must return home immediately after buying groceries, or the frozen foods will thaw, and dairy products may spoil. When you return home, have her put the groceries away, explaining that the frozen and refrigerated foods should be put away first, followed by other items that will not spoil. If you have bagged the frozen and refrigerated foods separately, this will be an easier task for her.

Clothing

As with supermarkets, discuss the stores that might be best to shop at. Large malls may be too confusing and overwhelming for her, so it may be best to select either smaller freestanding stores or those located in a strip mall. The advantage of starting to teach clothing shopping during adolescence is that she will probably shop at the same store for several years now that she is wearing adult sizes. Once you have decided on a store, use the same one repeatedly so that she becomes familiar with the layout and can find items more independently.

Before you actually start to shop, she needs to know what sizes she wears. What size does she wear for undergarments, shirts, pants, dresses, shoes, and so on? You will need to explain that although she wears a size 12 in pants, different styles and manufacturers have different cuts, and she may take a size 10 or 14 instead. The same issue will come up with shoe sizing. She may take a different size in athletic shoes versus dress shoes or sandals. Help her make up a card with all of her clothing sizes that she can keep in her wallet. That way, if she forgets a size, she can pull out the card while at the store.

An alternative to shopping in a physical store is to shop by catalog or on-line. This may become her shopping method of choice, particularly if a store whose merchandise she likes has an available catalog or an on-line presence. Most reputable stores who provide catalog or Internet shopping have excellent return policies. Many merchandisers actually include a return shipping label and instructions right in the package, or allow a return to one of their stores.

SUMMARY

As with everything, independent living skills must be specifically taught to the NLD child because she will not assimilate this information on her own.

There are four basic categories of independent living skills covered in this chapter: housekeeping, laundry, cooking, and shopping. A good time to begin teaching these skills is during adolescence when she is likely developmentally ready. However, start providing her with age-appropriate chores when she is much younger.

The following is a review of the highlights presented in each of the four independent living skill categories.

○ *Housekeeping* Teach the child to wash dishes manually, as well as how to use an electric dishwasher. When she is washing dishes manually, she should organize her work area, and use a basin set in the sink rather than put all of the dishes in a sink full of soapy water. Explain dangers such as glass breakage and sharp or pointed utensils which could cause injury. Show her how to load an electric dishwasher so that everything gets cleaned, and what settings to use. Teach her how to clean counters, bathrooms and appliances, and explain what cleaning agents to use. Provide instruction in the danger of toxic cleaning agents and the safeguards which are necessary. Teach her how to use a vacuum cleaner, and suggest that it be the all-purpose cleaner for dry floors. Show her how to use the various attachments, and explain what the buttons, knobs, and switches are. For wet floor cleaning, avoid a bucket which could be knocked over, and use a prepared cleanser in a spray bottle.

When dusting, make sure that she understands that not all dirt is visible, as well as the difference between spray waxes and spray solutions which make dusting more efficient. Teach her how to use a garbage disposal (if you have one), and dispose of garbage using plastic bags. Explain the details of recycling, and the schedule for trash pick-up. Teach her how to make a bed when she is younger, and change her sheets when she is an adolescent. Explain the dangers of changing light bulbs. Create a housekeeping schedule so that she can handle different tasks on different days in order to ensure that everything is done on a periodic basis, and to avoid her becoming overwhelmed. Write the various tasks on a monthly calendar and display it in a prominent place.

○ *Laundry* She will need to learn how to sort, wash, dry, and fold clothes, as well as understand what garments are to be dry-cleaned. Explain the 'care' tags that are sewn into garments which will assist her in determining washing and drying requirements. Teach her how to sort laundry based on color and fabric type, and what wash settings are appropriate for each item. Explain what items should be line dried and what can be put in an electric dryer, as well as the appropriate settings to be used. Show her how to fold laundry, beginning with the simple items (washcloths, towels), and provide a flat surface for her to work at.

° *Cooking* Teach her how to use a stove, microwave, and oven. When teaching her how to use the stove, begin with simple foods, such as a grilled-cheese sandwich. It would be helpful to use simple foods when introducing the microwave and oven also. An item such as prepared pizza is a good first choice because you can first teach her how to prepare it in the microwave, and then in the conventional oven. Baking can most readily be introduced using prepackaged cookies and cakes. Require her to use oven mitts so that she doesn't burn her hands or arms, and supervise her use of the stove and oven for an extended period since they are potentially dangerous appliances.

° *Shopping* Select a smaller grocery store that will not overwhelm her and teach her the layout, such as where the refrigerated foods, dry goods, and cleaning agents are located. Use a list when shopping, preferably ordered by the layout of the grocery store. Teach her how to bag groceries for weight and to avoid breaking (eggs) or squashing (bread) items, and bag refrigerated and frozen foods separately so that they can be put away first. Teach her what sizes she wears, and make a card with her clothing and shoe sizes on it that she can carry in her wallet. Select a small store, or one which is not in a large mall. Consider catalog and Internet shopping with reputable stores.

Chapter 13

Coping with Change

It should come as no surprise to read once again that NLD children thrive on routine and predictability, and deal poorly to horribly with change or novelty. Unfortunately, there are many situations in the NLD child's life that will be anxiety provoking, because they don't happen often enough for her to be able to develop a template. These children don't see the similarities in certain events, so they perceive many experiences as new, when in fact they are a new spin on an old experience. In order to help the child manage these experiences and begin to see the similarity between situations, you'll need to do some more work.

As you've no doubt seen, a trip to the doctor, the cancellation of a planned event, or a substitute teacher, may send this child into a panic or meltdown. The child's behavior is often misunderstood as manipulative or a simple temper tantrum. In the vast majority of situations, you will find that her response is because she has no means of coping with the change or event and figuratively or literally, she puts on the brakes.

In order for the child to manage something that to her is new or different, she needs preparation and lots of information. You'll need to let her know well ahead of time what the change or event will be, exactly when it will occur, the duration, and what will happen in detail. The following are common events and situations which may provoke anxiety in your child, along with suggestions for reducing her level of stress.

SEEING MEDICAL/HEALTH PROFESSIONALS
The pediatrician

A visit to the pediatrician will probably be quite stressful for this child. The entire event is confusing for her, and she may quickly become overwhelmed. A waiting room full of small children playing, darting about, and making noise is very disturbing, and the social challenges of being approached by other children to play will probably distress your child. After she has been escorted into an examining room, a nurse may weigh and measure her, take her blood pressure, and so forth. By the time the doctor actually sees the child, she may be on system overload. If she is seeing the doctor due to an illness, she will be even less able to handle the demands being placed on her.

When you schedule the appointment, explain that your child will have difficulty waiting in a noisy, crowded environment. Ask if you will be seen right away, or if you will have to wait. If there is a chance that you will have to wait, ask if there is a quiet place where you and your child can go, such as an empty examining room if the appointment is with a doctor. The ideal situation is to be seen immediately upon arrival so that the child doesn't become anxious while waiting; however, this may not be possible.

Arrange for the doctor to conduct the entire examination, rather than have the nurse do things such as check weight, height, and blood pressure. The pediatrician will need to take extra time with the child, be very patient, and take things slowly. If you have a good pediatrician who understands your child, this will be a given. For the young child, bring a favorite stuffed animal, and have the doctor show her what she will be doing at each step by first doing it to the stuffed animal with a full explanation, and then to the child. For the older child, the doctor needs to be very specific as to what she will do. 'I'm going to use this [as she displays the instrument] to look in your ears. It has a little light on the end so that I can see clearly. It may feel funny, but it won't hurt.' Each time that the child sees the doctor, she should explain again what she will do at each step. 'I'm going to use this to look in your ears. Do you remember that I did this the last time you were here? It didn't hurt, but it may feel funny.' Once the child and doctor develop a good rapport and the routine has been established, a simple 'remember this?' might suffice.

If you need to change to a new pediatrician, it would be helpful to make the appointment as outlined above so that you are either seen immediately, or can wait in a quiet place. The first appointment should be kept to just a few minutes – just enough time for the child to meet the doctor, chat briefly, see the environment and leave. This approach would be far less threatening to the child than being examined by a stranger in an unfamiliar setting.

Unfortunately, not every situation can be well orchestrated. The child may get sick and need to be seen by a covering pediatrician, or you may be away from home when she becomes ill. For these situations, do whatever you can to reduce the child's anxiety, or make it worth her while with a distraction such as a big fat bribe.

The dentist/orthodontist

Visits to the dentist or orthodontist can be very frightening, whatever the child's age. Sitting in that big chair which is reclined, a bright light in her eyes, all those instruments around her, the noise of a drill, the unusual odors, and the bib poking her in the neck. She's trapped, and the dentist wants her to open her mouth for who knows what reason.

Although many dentists now specialize in pediatrics, it doesn't automatically mean that it is the right place for your child. It would be best to select a small practice with private patient rooms, rather than a large open area with a lot of extraneous environmental distractions. Obviously, the dentist must be as patient and understanding as the pediatrician. Ideally, the doctor should do all of the work on the child, rather than involve a technician. However, if you must use a technician, be sure that it is always the same one, rather than being scheduled with the first available person. As with the pediatrician, the doctor and child need to develop a good rapport.

The child should probably begin to see a dentist when she is about four years old. Arrange a series of short visits to acclimatize her to the environment. On the first visit, have her simply meet the dentist, see the environment, and sit in the chair. The next visit, possibly at the interval that she will generally be seeing the dentist, might entail opening her mouth, and having one tooth cleaned. Gradually work up to a normal dental exam and cleaning. At every visit, the dentist will need to be very specific about what he will do before he does it, whether it's simply looking in her mouth, taking x-rays, or using the drain to keep her mouth dry while he works.

Orthodontic work is obviously more invasive than having your teeth cleaned or even having a cavity treated. Try and locate a doctor who has experience with developmentally disabled children. Your dentist should be aware of one, or should at least be able to recommend one who he thinks would have the experience and personality to respond to your child's needs. As with any other medical professional, if you find that your child is not comfortable with the orthodontist, find another because the situation probably won't improve. In the same way that the pediatrician and dentist must specifically explain what they are going to do, so must the orthodontist.

The psychologist/psychiatrist

In selecting a therapist for your child, make sure that he has experience with high functioning, developmentally disabled children. Traditional therapy, where patients share their feelings, doesn't work for NLD youngsters. This is commonly referred to as 'insight oriented' therapy. Since these children may have little or no insight, a more direct approach is required. It is worth looking until you find a therapist who is experienced with NLD (or a similar disorder, such as Asperger's syndrome). If possible, schedule a session to meet the doctor without bringing the child. Discuss what her needs are, and what you hope to accomplish. If you don't feel that the doctor understands the issues faced by an NLD child, then find another doctor. Once you have found a therapist who you and your child are comfortable with, he can be an invaluable support system, not only for your child, but for the entire family.

If the child is young, when you explain that she will be seeing this new person, it may be helpful to tell her that it is a 'talking' doctor, so that she understands that she won't be touched. Provide whatever information seems age-appropriate and non-threatening to her. For the older child, be very direct and honest. 'We are seeing a therapist to help us deal with your stress' (or anger, anxiety, depression – whatever her problem seems to be). Explain that this is someone who will listen to her, and work with her to find solutions to whatever is creating difficulty, and that she can even gripe about you!

Other medical professionals

Your child may see several other medical professionals, depending on her medical and health issues. Apply the strategies outlined above for the pediatrician, dentist/orthodontist and psychologist/therapist to the particular situation that you will be in. When you make the appointment, explain your child's NLD difficulties, and arrange for a quiet waiting area if you will not be seen immediately.

If possible, speak with the doctor ahead of time so that he knows what to expect with your child, and how to deal with her. Provide the child with as much advance information as possible, and at an age-appropriate level. Tell her how long it will take to get there, why you are going, and what to expect when you arrive. Make sure that the doctor explains everything to the child as her other doctors do.

VACATIONS

For most people, vacations are a time of fun and excitement. However, you may not find this with your NLD child. Remember that vacations may mean a change of routine and new experiences. Two of the most stressful events that may be related to a vacation are family trips and summer camp.

It is helpful to provide as much continuity with family trips as possible. For instance, if you like the water – either lake or ocean – consider renting the same cottage each year. This will provide a sense of security for the NLD child who becomes familiar with the environment through return visits, and has a certain level of understanding of what she can expect. Bring familiar things with you, such as her blanket, pillow, or any other special things that provide her comfort.

If your family prefers to go to different locations on each vacation, then consider staying at the same hotel chain. A good choice is Embassy Suites where the layout of the rooms is exactly the same from one location to the next. Although she will be in various locations, she will be reassured by the familiarity of the accommodations and services, such as breakfast in the hotel dining room, the swimming pool, possibly the video room, and of course the room itself.

Another advantage to staying at the same cottage or chain of hotels from one year to the next is that your child will be able to do things more independently. If staying at a hotel, make sure that she has her own key (assuming that she is old enough). Have her run simple errands for you – to get ice or a soft drink. Just these little things will give her a sense of independence and accomplishment.

When making a determination as to whether or not your child will attend summer camp, be as certain as possible that it is an experience that she will benefit from and enjoy. We tend to think that camp is a great adventure for our children, and one that they will all enjoy. For the NLD child, this may not be true. Although there is likely to be a schedule, and most or all activities will be supervised, camp tends to be a rather loosely structured and chaotic environment. She may also be required to take a bus to transport her to and from camp. The social demands and the lack of a defined structure may be overwhelming for her. If it is a residence camp, it may be wonderful, or hell, depending on the child. Yes, many youngsters are anxious about a camp experience, but remember that for the NLD child the anxiety, or a negative experience, may be too high a price for her to pay. Where other campers may be relaxed and enjoying themselves, she may be stressed to the max. Be sure to visit the camp ahead of time, discuss your child's needs with the camp director, and feel comfortable that they can support her. Have the child visit prior to beginning camp so that she can become somewhat familiar with the environment and the staff. Once she is there, reassure her that if she is having a difficult time, she can call and you will come and collect her.

A better choice for camp is to select one that caters to the special needs of learning disabled youngsters. Generally, you will find that they provide much more structure for the child, with a very high counselor to camper ratio, often one counselor to two or three campers. The counselors are specifically trained in the needs of the learning disabled camper, and are often special education teachers or university students majoring in the field of special needs children. Residence camps which cater to this population continue the high counselor to camper ratio in the cabins or dorms. This type of camp is specifically geared to creating a successful and rewarding experience for the learning disabled child.

An alternative to a private camp is your local town recreation department. Most towns have planned activities over the summer months, or even camps for residents. The more familiar environment and faces might make the experience more enjoyable for her. However, you should meet whoever will be coordinating your child's activities, and explain her needs. Just as with a private camp, you should feel comfortable with their ability to understand and support your child. To increase the likelihood that she will enjoy her experience, find out if a friend will be participating in any of the recreational activities, and schedule your child for the same camp sessions or events.

A final thought on vacation is to consider the fact that the child may need to use that time to recharge her batteries. She may insist on doing nothing all summer, and she might be right. School is incredibly stressful for her, and a quiet week during semester break, or even an entire summer of no demands may be exactly what she needs. We often consider that our children should do something meaningful with their time. In the case of the NLD child, meaningful may be a much-needed rest.

MOVING OR RELOCATING

Possibly the single most threatening change that the school-age NLD child could be faced with is moving from one home to another, or harder still, to a totally new location. When you tell her that you will be moving, wait for the fireworks – for they won't be long in coming. It is likely that she will scream and yell, rant and rave, from the time that you announce the move until well after you are in the new home. Most children will object to a move, but the NLD child's reaction will probably seem extreme. Considering how much difficulty she has in understanding the world around her, it is no wonder that she would react so poorly. Her security, possibly the only place that she feels safe, is being taken from her. If moving is an absolute necessity, plan it for the summer months when she is not in school. Expecting her to manage school demands and a move is unrealistic. Although you may not have a choice, understand the child's difficulty in dealing with it, and her likely reaction.

The above scenario assumes that the only change is from one home to another. If you are faced with a move to another area, the change will almost definitely be traumatic for the NLD child. Consider all of the things that she will have to adapt to:

- new home;
- new routine;
- new neighbors;
- new doctor;
- new dentist;
- new school;
- new teachers;
- new bus driver;
- new kids.

For the child who has difficulty managing change, you can understand why her reaction to a move might be so dramatic. You will need to spend considerable time helping her adjust to all of the newness, and establish whatever familiarity you can. Re-creating her new bedroom as closely to her old as possible might help. Continuing with a daily schedule which is as consistent as her old routine would also be beneficial. Gradually introduce her to new relationships with medical professionals. Take her to her new school when the children aren't there. Introduce her to her new teacher. Walk her through her schedule, and make her a simple map of the layout as we discussed earlier in this book. Make sure that you arrange for her to have a safe place to go when she becomes overwhelmed – whether that is the nurse's office, the guidance counselor, or the school psychologist – wherever she will receive the appropriate support. Be patient and understanding while she adjusts to her new world.

TRANSITIONS

Transitions in general will probably be difficult. The days preceding a semester break may be stressful as she anticipates the end of school, as will be the end of the school year. Obviously the days leading up to a return to school will be difficult as well. She may be anxious, or simply out of sorts. Talk with her about her concerns, whether they are specific or just a general anxiety about the change. If she seems to be quite anxious, it would be helpful to keep her occupied so that she has less time to worry about what might go wrong. Remember that many of her fears may be based on past negative experiences. Statements such as 'it will be fine, you'll see' may only heighten anxiety because you aren't being specific. WHY will things be fine? If you don't know that for a fact, it may be best to avoid clichés such as these.

Whenever your child is dealing with novelty, change and/or transition, look at the situation through her eyes. Understand that the world is a frightening place for her, and that she needs to know that you are there to protect and guide her. Her best long-term prognosis will depend on how safe and confident she feels under your care. Love what makes her unique – don't try to change her. Provide her with the tools that she will need in order to blossom into an independent and self-sufficient adult. She is a special child, as you are a special person, or God would not have selected you as her parent.

SUMMARY

There are many situations in the NLD child's life that will be anxiety provoking. Whether it's a trip to the doctor, dentist or orthodontist, psychologist or psychiatrist, or whether it's a move to another house or town, you will need to prepare the child as much as possible for these challenging situations.

When seeing the pediatrician, ask if there is a quiet place that you can wait, and arrange for the doctor to do the entire examination rather than involving a nurse. Have the doctor explain everything in detail before doing anything to the child, and consider first demonstrating on a stuffed animal for the younger child.

Start dental visits early, so that you can gradually ease the child into examinations and other dental procedures. Start small, with a simple visit to meet the dentist and sit in the chair, followed by a visit to clean just one tooth, and work forward from that point. If possible, avoid technicians, having the dentist do all of the child's dental work from cleaning her teeth, to taking x-rays, to treating a cavity. Select an orthodontist who has experience with developmentally disabled children, who have a lot in common with NLD youngsters.

When selecting a therapist, make sure that you find one who also has experience with developmentally disabled youngsters, preferably high-functioning children with disorders similar to NLD such as Asperger's syndrome. Insight-oriented therapy is not appropriate. A more direct therapeutic approach is required. Explain to the young child that this is a 'talking' doctor, and be honest with the older child. Tell her that you are seeing the therapist to discuss her problems and develop coping strategies.

Provide as much continuity for family trips as possible, either return to the same location (such as a cabin), or use the same hotel chain (such as Embassy Suites). This familiarity provides a sense of security for the child. Be cautious when selecting a camp, and consider camps which cater to learning disabled children. Always make sure that the camp director and counselors understand your child's needs.

Moving to a new house or a new location may be very frightening for your child. Re-create her old bedroom at the new location, and maintain a familiar schedule. Gradually expose her to new relationships such as the doctor and dentist. Prepare her for the new school by visiting when the children aren't there, have her meet the teacher, and show her the layout of the building.

Transitions of all kinds will probably cause stress. Understand how difficult they are for the child, and talk with her about her concerns. Avoid clichés such as 'It will be fine, you'll see.' Look at novelty, change and/or transition through her eyes and understand that the world is a frightening place for her. Her best long-term prognosis will depend on how safe and confident she feels under your care. Don't try and change her – love what makes her unique.

Chapter 14

Safety Issues

A concern shared by all parents is the physical and emotional safety of their children. For the parent of an NLD child, this will be an ongoing challenge, as the child is faced with various problems at different ages. When she is quite young, the dangers may include wandering off and getting lost, talking with strangers and/or getting hurt as a result of her lack of coordination. The older child may be faced with more insidious situations, such as drugs, alcohol, or even date rape, especially if she is allowed some level of independence and freedom.

PHYSICAL AND EMOTIONAL DANGERS

As youngsters, these children can turn a corner and be totally confused as to where they are or how they got there. Many don't have the skill to retrace their steps in order to find their way back to where they started. If she is separated from you in a mall or amusement park, an approach such as meeting at a designated location probably will not work, since the child may not be able to locate the designated spot.

The combination of the NLD child's naiveté, poor social judgment and strong language skill puts her at risk. She may answer the telephone, or open the door to a stranger, being open and honest with a person whom she has no reason to trust. If asked questions, in all likelihood she will answer truthfully, providing information such as her address, her age, the fact that she is alone, and so forth, assuming that it is safe to do so.

Unfortunately, their peer group often victimizes these children. At school, she may be teased, bullied, or even physically harmed by other children because of her differences or social ineptness. This is especially true in the upper elementary and middle school years when children tend to be less kind and accepting.

There is a very serious danger of the child being physically injured. Remember also that she won't readily learn cause and effect, or dangerous consequences, and not having learned from a previous experience, she may repeat something that has hurt her before. No matter how many times you tell this child that the stove is hot and will burn her, she might stick her hand right on the hot burner or in the flame. Or, she may be fascinated with the flames in a fireplace or wood-burning stove, and get too close, either being unaware of a safe distance or unable to recognize how close she actually is, or both. The child may climb a tree, not realizing that a branch can't hold her weight, and the branch may break under her. The older child may jump from an unsafe height, resulting in serious injury.

As the NLD child approaches or enters adolescence, the additional danger of being goaded by other children into risky or unacceptable behaviors and activities may become very troublesome. Whether it's encouraging her to make prank telephone calls or experiment with drugs and alcohol, peer pressure for these children can be quite dangerous.

Many NLD youngsters love the Internet, because the environment is totally word-dependent. She is able to initiate or respond to social contact using words, which is her comfort zone. Making social connections through the Internet may have advantages. The child may develop her social skills and make friends, which she would have difficulty doing in a face-to-face situation. However, this environment also has a serious risk for the NLD child. It leaves her vulnerable to predators who claim to be another child, or her 'friend,' both of which she may believe. She may be overjoyed with her new found 'friends' and unwittingly put herself in harm's way.

There is also the very, very real danger of these children being sexually exploited at all ages. NLD children want desperately to be accepted and are incredibly naive; they are therefore ripe for being the target of unsavory individuals. It is crucial that you remain vigilant with your child well into her teen years, and possibly beyond.

INTERVENTION
Safety at home

The following are some suggestions on how you might increase the safety of your NLD child in the home environment.

- ° If you have a young child and own your home, fence the yard, or at least the child's play area. This will prevent her from wandering off and becoming lost.

- ° If there are trees within the child's play area, cut the lower branches off so that she can't climb and either get stuck, or fall and injure herself.

- ° Keep your doors locked at all times, preferably with a key lock, to keep the child in and strangers out. That includes the door to your basement if you have one. These children can wander off and be quickly lost, or open the door to the basement and tumble down the stairs. Although somewhat expensive, an alarm system may provide additional safety for the child, and peace of mind for you.

- ° Use kiddy gates to prevent the younger child from getting near unsafe areas of the house, such as a fireplace, wood-burning stove, or kitchen stove that is turned on. This might continue longer than with a neurologically typical child due to this child's difficulty understanding cause and effect, and not learning from previous experience.

○ This child may turn on the hot water to wash her hands or take a shower without first adjusting the temperature to an acceptable level. Adjust the temperature on your hot water tank so that the child will not seriously burn herself.

○ Consider some type of protective device to surround the stove burners, or raised fireplace hearth so that they can't touch hot burners or tip over a pot with scalding contents, or fall against the sharp edge of a fireplace hearth.

Safety outside the home

The following are some suggestions on how you might increase the safety of your NLD child outside of the home environment.

○ Never leave this child in a car unattended. There are numerous risks associated with an unattended child. This applies well into adolescence, and possibly beyond. Yes, this is true for all children, but much more so for the NLD child. If the child is spatially challenged, and decides that she wants to leave the car to find you, she may become hopelessly lost, or get injured.

○ As your child is allowed to leave the yard to play within the neighborhood, make sure that you know exactly where she is at all times. Walk her to the destination, or have the receiving parent call as soon as the child arrives, and again when she leaves to come home. Teach the child that she is not to go elsewhere unless she specifically checks with you first.

○ Don't allow the child to ride her bicycle on a busy street. Her poor sense of space and direction could cause her to become involved in an accident, or get seriously lost. This applies right into her teen years.

◦ Teach the child what to do in the event that you become separated in a crowded public place such as a shopping mall or amusement park. If employees wear a specific type of uniform, point it out to the child, and tell them to go to a person with that uniform on if they need help. If there is no uniform, tell the child to go to an employee who is behind a counter or at a cash register to get assistance. If neither is available to the child, suggest that she approach a woman who is with children, and ask for her help. Be very specific about who the child should approach for assistance.

◦ To allow the older child more freedom, provide her with a walkie-talkie so that she can contact you if need be. This also allows you to keep in touch with her, and always know where she is. A walkie-talkie is also very beneficial if you are going to be with the child in a large public area, whether it is the mall or an amusement park. If you become separated, or if you want to allow the older child a bit of independence, the walkie-talkie will allow you to maintain contact.

◦ For the adolescent and teen, provide her with a cell-phone when she is away from the house. Make sure that she checks in with you on a predetermined schedule, and if she doesn't, then call her. This may seem like an expensive strategy, but it will allow more independence while providing a safety net in the event that the child finds herself in a difficult situation. Consider the circumstances that may be avoided, such as date rape, or being abandoned by friends with no way to get home. Unfortunately, many parents feel that this will never happen to their child…and then it does, with disastrous results. When comparing the cost to the potential danger, a cell-phone is actually a small price to pay to ensure your child's safety. Also keep in mind that cell-phones have become more affordable, and will become even more inexpensive in the coming years.

Safety with others

The following are some suggestions on how you might increase the safety of your NLD child in situations where they are dealing with others.

- ° Make sure that you know all of your child's friends, assuming that she has some. Get to know the parents so that you can determine whether the friend is an appropriate role model, and whether the parent supervises the children's activities. This applies to older children as well. For instance, does the parent accompany the children to the movies or mall, or simply drop them off?

- ° Know the older child's acquaintances as well, and investigate any new relationships. Again, you want to know that the individual is an appropriate role model. You also need to know the age and gender of all of your child's acquaintances. It is not appropriate for a naive adolescent girl to have a 19-year-old male friend.

- ° Teach the young child that NO ONE is to touch her on certain parts of her body, OR tell her to undress unless you (or some other designated adult) are with her. Although a rule this rigid could create certain inconveniences, such as a teacher or another parent checking for an injury if she is hurt, it is still the best protection for your child. She generally doesn't understand shades of gray, so it is best to provide a steadfast rule rather than to expect her to determine what is appropriate and what isn't.

- ° All children need specific instruction regarding the risks of talking with or going somewhere with strangers. However, the NLD child needs more instruction than other children. She will not have the instinctive 'feeling' that someone isn't to be trusted, or discomfort with a particular situation. It is wise to err on the side of caution when it comes to your child's safety. If you hear even a hint of a negative rumor about a particular parent or teacher, do not expose your child to them.

Safety at school

Make sure that one specific adult is assigned to the safety and well-being of your child when she is at school. If circumstances warrant, have that adult monitor your child during all unstructured periods – whether it is between classes, at recess, in the cafeteria, on the school bus – wherever she may be at risk for teasing, bullying, or other peer victimization.

FINAL THOUGHTS

It is impossible to anticipate all of the potential dangers which your child may face. It is important to be vigilant, and aware that your child will likely not develop the 'street smarts' that other children seem to acquire. Unfortunately, her innocence may often be used against her. Although her coordination will likely improve with age, her spatial challenges may persist. The risk of becoming lost and resulting in harm increases as her world expands. You will need to 'over protect' this child in order to ensure her safety.

We cannot and should not prevent our children from growing up, even knowing that the danger to them will increase with age. The fact is that this is true with all children. However, for the NLD child, the dangers are more pervasive. As your child is exposed to new situations, always ask yourself, 'What risk does this situation pose, and how can I mitigate the danger?' Trust your instincts, and don't bow to external pressure from well-intentioned people who tell you that you worry too much.

SUMMARY

Protecting the NLD child from physical and emotional harm will be an ongoing challenge. The younger child may get lost, talk with strangers, or get hurt due to her lack of coordination. The older child is a target for peer victimization and vulnerable to predators. Poor social judgment at all ages creates the potential for danger. The Internet has social advantages, but be aware of the disadvantages.

Protect the younger child from physical harm by locking all doors or using an alarm system, fencing the yard, cutting lower branches from trees, using kiddy gates, and never leaving her unattended in a car. Prevent injury by adjusting the hot-water heater temperature, and protect the child from a wood-burning stove, fireplace and hearth, as well as a hot stove.

Make sure that you know where the child is at all times, either accompanying her to and from a friend's house or, for the older child, have the receiving parent call when she has arrived, and again when she is preparing to come home. Never allow the child to ride her bicycle on a busy street.

Teach the child what to do in the event you become separated in a public place such as a shopping mall or amusement park. A walkie-talkie may provide more freedom for the child, while still maintaining contact. A cell-phone is a very important safety tool for the NLD adolescent and teen. Know all of your child's friends and acquaintances. Investigate any new relationships, especially if she met them through the Internet. This child needs positive role models, and is vulnerable to predators.

Establish a rigid rule about touching and undressing so that the child is not expected to determine what is and is not appropriate. Drill this child on the rules of talking or going somewhere with strangers. Protect the child from anyone who could be a risk. Provide rigid rules for Internet activities, and always monitor your child when she is on-line. Have your child's school assign a specific adult to ensure that your child is not exposed to peer victimization.

Ask yourself, 'What risk does this situation pose, and how can I mitigate the danger?'

Afterword

The Miracle of Music

Although there have been no formal studies regarding a connection between NLD and musical ability, a large percentage of these children seem to have a talent in this area. Some have perfect pitch, while others have talent with instruments.

Several years ago our neuropsychologist encouraged us to have our daughter take drum lessons. Since I am not a musician, I don't recall all the reasons that drums in particular were recommended, although I do remember her telling me that we should continue to encourage activities which stimulate the right hemisphere. Apparently, music lessons and/or playing an instrument do that.

Three years later, I am astounded with the difference music has made for our daughter. Not only has she become an accomplished drummer, but she plays electric, acoustic, and bass guitar. Each has benefited her in different ways.

When she started drum lessons, it was all very awkward and frustrating. However, with practice and an excellent instructor, she grasped the 'feel' of the instrument fairly quickly. After two years of playing drums, we see the following benefits:

- ° she now comfortably crosses midline;

- ° she is far more coordinated and spatially aware;

- ○ she is far more physically fit;

- ○ her thinking skills have improved;

- ○ her problem solving skills have improved;

- ○ her handwriting speed has improved;

- ○ her self-esteem is much better;

- ○ her confidence as a musician is established;

- ○ she has a physical outlet for her anger and frustration.

She also plays electric and acoustic guitar quite well. Because of her interest in music, she was encouraged to play with a group at her school each week during chapel. As a result of this activity, she has come out of her shell, further improved her confidence and self-esteem, and is more accepted by the other students. If someone had told me two years ago that my child would get up in front of an audience for any purpose, I would have said no way! Historically, she has been terrified of being the center of attention, and is naturally quite shy. However, when she is playing her music, a metamorphosis occurs – she becomes a different person.

Bass guitar was added to her repertoire about a year ago. She picked it up quite naturally, apparently because it is a percussion instrument, as are drums. Not long after beginning lessons, a young group of boys contacted her to play in their band. As it turns out, the band is quite talented, both as individual musicians, and as a group. They have played twice at a local coffee house, and were quite happily paid for their gigs. And, they have been asked back for a third engagement. She's 15 years old, as are most of the boys in the band, and she's never been happier in her life. She's finally really good at something, and being recognized for it. Some of the kids who have been unkind to her in the past are stunned at what she has accomplished. Recently, after hearing her play, one young man said, 'Stef, I didn't know you had it in you!' Being involved in the band has drawn her out even more. She asserts her opinion about their music, and what she wants to do to improve it. The boys respect her and her opinions. It is truly a joy to behold. The 'fly in the ointment' is that she won't let her father or me watch her perform. As you can imagine, restraint has been a challenge for both of us, but I respect Stef's wishes, at least for the moment. I'm happy being happy for her.

The reason that I chose to share this with you is because finding something that the child can do, and do well, is terribly important. The benefits we have seen from music are immeasurable, and I would encourage any parent of an NLD child to pursue music, drama, art, or whatever taps into your child's passion. Every time I get a headache from listening to our daughter practice the drums, I remember to smile and be thankful, and wish the same for you.

Appendix I

Glossary of Terms

Abstract thinking
The ability to think in terms of ideas or concepts rather than facts.

Accommodations
Adaptations or adjustments provided to fit the particular needs of an individual because of their disability.

Achievement test
A test in core curriculum areas, such as reading or mathematics, to determine a student's level of academic achievement.

Agenesis of Corpus Callosum
Agenesis of Corpus Callosum (ACC) is a rare disorder that is present at birth. It is characterized by a partial or complete absence (agenesis) of an area of the brain that connects the two cerebral hemispheres. This part of the brain is normally composed of transverse fibers. Agenesis of Corpus Callosum is usually inherited as either an autosomal recessive trait or an X-linked dominant trait. It can also be caused by an infection during the twelfth to the twenty-second week of pregnancy (intrauterine) leading to developmental disturbance of the fetal brain. In some cases mental retardation may result, but in other cases, no evident symptoms may appear and intelligence may not be impaired.

Alternate assessment
An evaluation process which uses non-traditional testing methods to assess a student's ability and/or knowledge which is appropriate to their specific needs and accommodates their disability.

Amygdala
A region in the forebrain involved in integrating and coordinating emotional behaviors.

Anosognosia
A lack of comprehension or awareness in an individual of the extent of their disabilities and limitations.

Asperger's syndrome (AS)
A developmental disability characterized by normal intelligence, motor clumsiness, eccentric interests and a limited ability to appreciate social nuances.

Assistive technology device
Any item, piece of equipment, or other device, which is acquired commercially off the shelf, modified, or customized, which is used to increase, maintain, or improve functional capabilities of a child with a disability.

Assistive technology service
Any service that directly assists a child with a disability in the selection, acquisition, or use of an assistive technology device.

Association areas
Regions of the cerebral cortex concerned with higher levels of processing.

Association neurons
Cells that mediate interactions between neurons.

Attention Deficit Disorder (ADD)
A neurologically based condition which is characterized by distractedness, short attention span and impulsiveness.

Autism
A developmental disability, with onset in infancy or early childhood, characterized by severe deficits in social responsiveness and interpersonal relationships, abnormal speech and language development, and repetitive or stereotyped behaviors.

Autoreceptors
Receptors found on synaptic terminals that are activated by the substances released by the terminals.

Axon
That part of the neuron that sends information away from the cell body.

Axon terminals
Branches of an axon near its site of termination. Synapses (see entry) are typically made by axon terminals.

Behavioral Intervention Plan (BIP)
A written intervention plan for a student whose behavior significantly interferes with his or her learning and/or the other students' opportunity to learn.

Bilateral integration
The harmonious working relationship between the two sides of the body.

Body image
An abstract internal representation of spatial and physical-mechanical properties of one's body (including muscle, skeleton, organs, and so on).

Broca's area
An area (usually found in the left frontal lobe of the cerebral cortex) critical for the production of language.

Central nervous system
Consists of the brain and spinal cord.

Cerebellum
A prominent hindbrain structure important for coordinating and integrating motor activity.

Cerebral cortex
A layer of cells that covers the forebrain. Highly infolded in man, the cortex is divided into two hemispheres, which are further subdivided into four lobes – frontal, parietal, occipital, and temporal.

Closure
Bringing together to form a conclusion – or the 'whole' as it relates to the 'parts' of a concept or situation.

Compensations
Alternative solutions or strategies to accommodate a disability in order to remove barriers created by the disability.

Comprehension
The act or ability of understanding – to get the meaning.

Congenital hypothyroidism
Congenital hypothyroidism is a condition characterized by abnormally decreased activity of the thyroid gland and deficient production of thyroid hormones present at birth. The thyroid gland secretes hormones that play an essential role in regulating growth, maturation and the rate of metabolism.

Coordination
The harmonious working together of muscle groups in performing complex movements.

Corpus callosum
A thick band of axons found in the middle of the brain that carries information from one side of the brain to the other.

Crystallized intelligence
Storehouse of general information or knowledge; over-learned skills; rote learning; information based on past learning.

de Lange syndrome
Cornelia de Lange syndrome (CdLS) is a rare genetic disorder that is apparent at birth. Associated symptoms and findings typically include delays in physical development before and after birth. There are characteristic abnormalities of the head and facial area which result in a distinctive facial appearance. In addition, there are malformations of the hands and arms, with mild to severe mental retardation.

Dendrites
Bushy branch-like structures that extend from the cell body of a neuron and receive the synaptic input to the cell.

Development
The process of maturational growth.

Directionality
The projection of laterality (developed within oneself; see entry) to outside oneself.

Discrimination
The ability to differentiate between two or more sensory stimuli.

Diskinesia
An impairment of voluntary movement, resulting in fragmented or incomplete movements; poor coordination.

DSM-IV
Diagnostic and Statistical Manual, (fourth edn) (American Psychiatric Association).

Dysgraphia
A disability of the physical act of printing or cursive handwriting.

Dyssemia
Difficulty in using and understanding nonverbal signs and signals; a nonverbal communication deficit.

Echolalia
The apparent meaningless repetition of exact words or phrases spoken by another, then used in place of original speech.

Encephalopathy
A brain disorder, especially one involving alterations of brain structure.

Etiology
The cause or source of a syndrome or disease.

Fetal Alcohol Syndrome

Fetal Alcohol Syndrome (FAS) is a characteristic pattern of birth defects that result due to maternal use of alcohol during pregnancy. The range and severity of associated symptoms and findings may be extremely variable from case to case. Affected infants and children may have learning and behavioral abnormalities, such as increased irritability during infancy, mild to severe mental retardation, short attention span, poor judgment, and impulsiveness.

Fine motor skills

The use of small muscle groups for specific tasks such as handwriting.

Finger agnosia

The inability to recognize and interpret sensory impressions with fingers (generally the finger tips), caused by an impairment in the brain.

504 plan

Section 504 of PL 93-112 (the Rehabilitation Act of 1973), as it applies to an individual's right to education, requires that a 504 Plan or an IEP be developed to remove the barriers to learning. All students who qualify under IDEA also qualify under 504. However, the reverse is not always true. Not all students who qualify under 504 also qualify under IDEA.

Fluid intelligence

Practical, hands-on intelligence; how well a person 'thinks on their feet'; how quickly and competently a person processes and utilizes the information at his or her disposal.

Forebrain

The most distal part of the brain, consisting principally of the thalamus, hypothalamus, basal ganglia, and cerebral cortex.

Free appropriate public education

Special education and related services that have been provided at public expense, under public supervision and direction, and without charge. Such services meet the standards of the state educational agency; include an appropriate preschool, elementary, or secondary school program in the state involved, and are provided in conformity with the individualized education program required by federal law.

Frontal lobe

The most anterior portion of the cerebral cortex, concerned primarily with movement and smell.

Frontloading

Providing 'preview' materials to a student prior to the actual instruction of a unit or topic of study.

Full inclusion

A placement in which a special education student receives instruction within the regular classroom setting for the entire school day.

Gestalt perception

Deriving meaning from the 'whole picture,' without breaking it down into parts; 'putting it all together'; having a holistic view.

Glia

Supporting cells in the brain that help maintain neurons, regulate the environment, and form the myelin (see entry) around axons.

Gray matter

Those regions of the brain and spinal cord where neuronal cell bodies and dendrites (see entry) are abundant.

Guidepost neurons

Specialized cells found in the developing brain that guide axonal growth.

Hand–eye coordination

The integration of visual and tactile systems which enables the hand to be used as a tool of the visual processes.

Hard signs (neurological)

Unequivocal, medically documented signs of brain damage, such as brain surgery, cerebral bleeding, hemiplegia, brain tumor, or penetrating head injury (see also 'Soft signs' entry).

Hearing impairment

A permanent or fluctuating hearing loss that significantly hinders educational performance.

Hemisphere (cortical)

Half of the cerebral cortex. The two cortical hemispheres are each subdivided into four lobes.

Hydrocephalus

A condition in which abnormally widened (dilated) cerebral spaces in the brain (ventricles) inhibit the normal flow of cerebrospinal fluid (CSF). The cerebrospinal fluid accumulates in the skull and puts pressure on the brain tissue.

Hyperlexia

A syndrome which interferes with speech, language, and social interaction. It may be accompanied by unusual or 'different' behaviors. Children exhibit an intense fascination with letters, numbers, patterns, logos, and so on, and a very precocious ability to read, spell, write and/or compute from as early as 18 months to before the age of five.

Hypothalamus

A forebrain region that contains nuclei concerned with basic acts and drives such as eating, drinking, and sexual activity. The hypothalamus also regulates the release of pituitary gland hormones and the autonomic nervous system, and plays an important role in emotional behavior.

Hypotonia

A condition characterized by decreased muscle tone that is manifested as muscle weakness or 'floppiness.' The condition can occur as a disorder of unknown cause, or as a symptom of other neuromuscular diseases.

Impairment

A neurological blockage or barrier to expected development.

Inclusive schooling

Educating all children, with and without disabilities, together. Materials are adapted, modified, and changed to accommodate the needs of individual students. Inclusive schooling allows disabled students to exercise their basic right to be educated in the same educational environment as their peers.

Individualized Education Plan (IEP)

An IEP is a written document stating a student's present levels of performance, disability, educational goals, modifications, and kind and level of services to be provided. Every IEP must be approved by a pupil planning team consisting of several members, including a school administrator, a special education teacher, and the student's parent.

Individualized Transition Plan (ITP)

A specific and formalized plan which addresses the issues necessary for a student's transition from high school to work, college or university, or community living, and who qualify for special education services under PL 92-142 (IDEA).

Inference

Going beyond available evidence to form a conclusion.

Integration

A placement in which a special education student receives instruction within the regular classroom setting for the entire school day.

Intervention

The therapeutic and/or educational methods employed to aid a child once a disability has been diagnosed.

Intervention-based multifactored evaluation

A collaborative, problem solving process which focuses upon concerns which affect the learner's educational progress within a learning environment.

Kinesthesia
The sensory knowledge and awareness of the body and body parts in space; includes awareness of balance and motion.

Laterality
The internal awareness individuals have of the two sides of their body.

Least restrictive environment
A term from PL92-142 (IDEA) requiring that, to the greatest extent possible, students with disabilities must be educated with their non-disabled peers.

Long-term memory
Memories that last for long periods – weeks, months, or longer.

Low incidence disability
A severely disabling condition with an expected incidence rate of less than one percent of the total statewide enrollment for kindergarten through grade 12 students.

Mainstreaming
Placing students with special needs in regular classroom settings with support services.

Midline
An imaginary line marking the middle of the body, running from head to toe, separating the right from the left side of the body.

Mind blindness
The inability to take the perspective of another.

Modality
A sensory mode (that is auditory, visual, tactile, kinesthetic) used by an individual to process information.

Monoamine
A type of substance released at synapses that functions mainly as a neuromodulator.

Myelin
An insulating layer of membrane formed around axons – much like insulation around electrical wires.

Neuromodulator
Substance released at a synapse that causes biochemical changes in a neuron.

Neurons
Cells in the brain involved in the reception, integration, and transmission of signals.

Neurotransmitter
Substance released at a synapse that causes fast electrical excitation or inhibition of a neuron.

Obsess

To fill the mind (keep the attention of) to an unreasonable or unhealthy extent.

Obsessive compulsive disorder

Obsessive compulsive disorder is characterized by recurrent habitual obsessive or compulsive thoughts or actions. These obsessions and compulsions may become very distressing and time-consuming. In severe cases they can significantly interfere with a person's normal routine, occupational functioning, usual social activities or relationships with others.

Occipital lobe

The most posterior portion of the cerebral cortex, concerned with visual processing.

Occupational therapy

The purpose of occupational therapy is to improve, develop, or restore functions impaired or lost through illness, injury, or deprivation; to improve an individual's ability to perform tasks for independent functioning if those functions are lost or impaired; through early intervention, to prevent the initial or further impairment or loss of function.

Orbitofrontal cortex

An area found in the lower part of the frontal lobes, important for the expression of emotional behaviors.

Parietal lobe

Region of the cerebral cortex between the frontal and occipital lobes concerned primarily with somatosensory information processing.

Perception

The process by which patterns of environmental energies become known as objects, events, people, and other aspects of the world – insight, comprehension.

Perceptual motor disability

Difficulty using a utensil. Problems with clarity of handwriting, letter formation, inconsistent pencil pressure, and so on.

Peripheral nervous system

Parts of the nervous system outside of the brain and spinal cord.

Perseverate

To continue or repeat an action after the stimulus or need for it has passed.

Physical therapy

The health specialty which addresses the prevention of physical disability as well as the habilitation or rehabilitation of physical disabilities, either congenital or acquired, resulting from, or secondary to, injury or disease.

Position emission tomography (PET) scanning
A method for detecting increases in activity of a part of the brain.

Pragmatics
The relation between signs or linguistic expressions and their users (functional use of language).

Primary motor area
The region of the cerebral cortex where fine movements are initiated. Found in the frontal lobes adjacent to the central sulcus.

Primary sensory area
Regions where sensory information is first processed in the cerebral cortex.

Proprioceptive information
Sensory information from muscles, joints, and tendons of which we are not conscious.

Prosody
Tone, accent, modulation, and all other characteristics of speech.

Psychomotor
Muscular activity which is directly related to, or resulting from, mental processes – the brain controlling movement.

Pyramidal cell
A prominent neuron found in all areas of the cerebral cortex.

Related services
Non-academic services which a child requires in order to receive a free appropriate public education (see entry). Examples of these services may be special transportation, speech-language pathology and audiology services, counseling services and others which are determined to be necessary by the pupil planning team of the disabled student.

Schizophrenia
A severe mental disease characterized by thought and mood disorders, hallucinations, and so on.

Semantic Pragmatic Disorder
A communication disorder with mild autistic symptoms and problems generalizing information.

Semantics
The study of meanings in language – connotative meaning.

Sensorimotor
Having to do with both sensory and motor activity in the body.

Sensory integration

The brain's ability to take in and synthesize multi-modality experiences perceived by the senses (vision, hearing, smell, taste, touch, motion, and temperature).

Sensory integration therapy (SIT)

An occupational therapy treatment program consisting of exercises which encourage the individual to use as many nerve–cell connections as possible.

Serotonin

A substance released at synapses that most often acts as a neuromodulator. Decreased levels of serotonin in the brain have been linked to depression.

Short-term memory

The initial storage of information. Short-term memories are unstable and easily disrupted.

Social perceptual disability

A disability characterized by the inability effectively to use non-verbal cues in a social setting.

Soft signs (neurological)

Behavioral deviations identified by a neurologist, where a traditional neurological examination does not reveal hard signs (see entry) of brain damage or dysfunction. These indications (including poor directional sense, neuromuscular clumsiness, and others) are strongly suggestive of abnormal functioning of the central nervous system.

Sotos syndrome

Sotos syndrome is a rare genetic disorder characterized by excessive growth prior to and after birth. Children affected by Sotos syndrome may exhibit characteristic facial differences and developmental delays. The syndrome is also called Cerebral Gigantism.

Specific learning disability

As defined in the Individuals with Disabilities Education Act (IDEA), a specific learning disability means a disorder in one or more of the basic psychological processes involved in understanding or in using language (spoken or written), which may manifest itself in an imperfect ability to listen, think, speak, read, write, spell, or to do mathematical calculations.

Speech-language pathologist (SLP)

A professional educated and trained in the study of human communication, its development and its disorders.

Speech-language therapy

The treatment of speech and language disorders (not limited to articulation problems), including deficits in pragmatic language.

Strategies
Defined plans or methods employed towards a goal.

Synapse
The site of functional contact between two neurons or a neuron and muscle cell.

Syndrome
A cluster of signs and symptoms which, considered together, are characteristic of a particular disease or disorder.

Tactile
Of or having to do with the sense of touch.

Tactile perception
How an individual interprets the things he or she feels or touches.

Tactile-kinesthetic
Relating to the sense of touch and the feeling of movement – touching and doing.

Temporal lobe
The lateral-most part of the cerebral cortex, concerned with hearing and memory.

Thalamus
A forebrain region that relays sensory information to the cerebral cortex.

Tourette syndrome
Tourette syndrome is a hereditary neurological movement disorder that is characterized by repetitive motor and vocal tics. Symptoms may include involuntary movements of the extremities, shoulders, and face accompanied by uncontrollable sounds and, in some cases, inappropriate words.

Turner syndrome
Turner syndrome is a rare chromosomal disorder of females characterized by short stature and the lack of sexual development at puberty. Other physical features may include a webbed neck, heart defects, kidney abnormalities, and/or various other malformations.

Velocardiofacial syndrome
Velocardiofacial syndrome is a rare genetic disorder characterized by abnormalities of the head and facial area, heart defects that are present at birth, diminished muscle tone, mild small stature, mental retardation, slight delays in the acquisition of skills requiring the coordination of mental and muscular activities (psychomotor retardation) and/or learning disabilities.

Visual discrimination
Visual adeptness at perceiving similarities and differences in geometric figures, symbols, pictures, and words.

Visual motor

The relationship between visual input and motoric output, as in copying text.

Visual motor integration

The coordination of visual information with motor processes.

Visual perception

How an individual interprets the things he or she sees.

Visualization

The ability to picture and manipulate visual images within one's mind.

Visuo-spatial

Of the field of vision, particularly as it involves the relationships of space and configuration of the object seen.

Wernicke's area

An area in the left temporal lobe concerned with the comprehension of language, reading and writing.

White matter

Areas of the brain where there is an abundance of myelinated axons. The myelin sheath consists of a light, colored fatty substance which gives the tissue its whitish appearance.

Williams syndrome

A developmental disorder affecting connective tissue and the central nervous system. Characteristics of this disorder include heart disease, dysmorphic facial features, and poor visual-motor integration.

WISC-III

Wechsler Intelligence Scale for Children (third edn). Five subtests make up the verbal scale, and five subtests make up the performance scale. The WISC-III provides three IQ scores: verbal, performance, and full scale.

Working memory

A memory maintained for a short time to enable a specific task to be accomplished, such as remembering a telephone number until it is dialed.

Appendix II

Annotated Bibliography

Anatomy Coloring Workbook, I. Edward Alcamo, 1997, Princeton Review
Publishing, LLC (ISBN 0-679-77849-87)
> The author presents a unique approach to learning the human anatomy, using a
> step-by-step instructional strategy, requiring the reader to use a coloring process
> as they learn. The section on the nervous system is particularly valuable to anyone
> who wants to develop a better understanding of disease or dysfunction affecting
> the brain. This is a fun way to tackle a complex topic.

Asperger Syndrome: A Guide for Parents and Professionals, Tony Attwood,
1998, Jessica Kingsley Publishers (ISBN 1-85302-577-1)
> This is an excellent book on Asperger's syndrome that would also be very
> interesting to the NLD population. As you read the book, at times you will forget
> that you are reading about Asperger's syndrome since much of what the author
> covers relates incredibly well to NLD. This is an easy, quick read, and you'll enjoy
> the author's compassion and wit.

*Attention Deficit Disorder and Learning Disabilities: Realities, Myths and
Controversial Treatments*, Barbara D. Ingersoll and Sam Goldstein, 1993,
Doubleday (ISBN 0-38546-931-4)
> This is a readable and informative overview of ADD and learning disabilities,
> with a section on NLD (referred to as 'visual-motor learning disability'). This
> book is treatment-oriented, including alternative therapies of which the authors
> largely disapprove.

The Blackwell Dictionary of Cognitive Psychology, Michael W. Eysenck (ed), Andrew Ellis, Earl Hunt and Philip Johnson-Laird (advisory eds), 1990, Blackwell (ISBN 0-631-15682-8 hardback; ISBN 0-631-19257-3 paperback)

> This book contains 140 encyclopedia-style entries on topics in contemporary cognitive psychology. There are also suggestions for further reading on each topic, and a comprehensive and helpful index. This is an easy to use book which would be helpful for individuals looking for the 'thumbnail sketch' descriptions on topics ranging from body image to the pragmatics of language to nonverbal communication. An excellent resource.

Brain Repair, Donald G. Stein, Simon Brailowsky and Bruno Will, 1995, Oxford University Press (ISBN 0-19-511918-5)

> The authors of this book are neuroscientists who present in lay terms the advances being made in brain research. They discuss the concept of brain plasticity, and explain how the brain manufactures a number of chemicals that foster growth and repair damaged neurons.

Child Neuropsychology: Assessment and Interventions for Neuropsychiatric and Neurodevelopmental Disorders of Childhood, Phyllis Anne Teeter and Margaret Semrud-Clikeman, 1997, Allyn & Bacon (ISBN 0-20516-331-9)

> The authors present the most current information regarding the influences of brain function on the cognitive-perceptual, learning, behavioral, and psychosocial adjustment of children and adolescents. The intended audience is professionals working in the field of child/adolescent psychology.

Comic Strip Conversations, Carol Gray, 1994, Future Horizons (ISBN 1-885-47722-8)

> The creator of 'social stories' has expanded the concept through the use of what she refers to as 'comic strip conversations.' This concept uses a simple, but effective, illustrative process to teach social and communication skills to children with developmental disabilities.

Communication Disorders and Interventions in Low Incidence Pediatric Populations, Lisa Schoenbrodt and Romayne A. Smith, 1995, Singular Publishing Group (ISBN 1-565932-20-X)

> In this book, the authors present the medical background, etiology, characteristics, assessment and intervention of various neurological conditions. Specific conditions addressed include traumatic brain injury, fragile X syndrome, autism, and pervasive developmental disorders.

Cooking Made Easy, Eileen Laird, 1996, Cookbook Publishers (may be purchased through author's website at *www.cookingmadeeasy.org*)

> This book is a great resource for teaching individuals with NLD how to cook. The author assumes no cooking knowledge, and the directions are incredibly specific, including information such as size of bowl needed, what utensil to use and what part of vegetables to keep and which to throw away.

Creating Mind: How the Brain Works, John E. Dowling, 1998, W.W. Norton and Co. (ISBN 0-393-02746-5)

> The first half of this book covers the nuts and bolts necessary for an up-to-date understanding of the brain. The remainder of the book examines aspects of brain function – vision, perception, language, memory, emotion, and consciousness – that are more directly relevant to how the brain creates mind. It is an excellent handbook for the layperson who wants to develop a better understanding of the brain.

Developmental Dyspraxia: A Practical Manual for Parents and Professionals, Madeleine Portwood, 1996, Durham County Council (ISBN 1-897585-21-7)

> The topic of this book is developmental dyspraxia which is a neurological disorder bearing a striking resemblance to characteristics of NLD. There is a very interesting and easy to understand chapter on the development and function of the brain, as well as suggested intervention strategies for both the early years and the older student.

Emotional Intelligence: Why It Can Matter More Than IQ, Daniel Goleman, 1995, Bantam Books (ISBN 0-553-09503-X)

> The author challenges the current emphasis on cognitive and academic intelligence, and suggests that emotional maturity, social judgment, etc. (deficit areas for individuals with NLD), may play a greater role in determining success in life.

The Explosive Child: A New Approach for Understanding and Parenting Easily Frustrated, 'Chronically Inflexible' Children, Ross W. Greene, (ed) 1998, HarperCollins (ISBN 0-06017-534-6)

> The author devotes an entire chapter to describing NLD children, and points out that inflexibility and low tolerance for frustration are major issues with this disorder. He suggests that the behavior of children who are inflexible and easily frustrated is not manipulative or purposeful, but rather a result of developmental deficits.

Hearing Equals Behavior, Guy Berard, (Foreword by Bernard Rimland and Afterword by Annabel Stehli), 1993, Keats Publishing
(ISBN 0-87983-600-8)
> This book is authored by the pioneer of auditory integration training (AIT) in which he clearly and simply describes the auditory system of brain function. He goes on to outline disorders which may benefit from AIT, as well as what the treatment consists of. Although this book is out of print, it is worth reading if you are able to locate it.

Helping The Child Who Doesn't Fit In, Stephen Nowicki, Jr., and Marshall P. Duke, 1992, Peachtree Publishers (ISBN 1-56145-025-1)
> Nowicki and Duke explain how nonverbal behavior affects a child's social competence and acceptance. The authors describe nonverbal communication as a 'language' of its own, and suggest methods of teaching children the meaning of things such as space and touch, gestures and postures, facial expressions and other necessary components of communication.

Helping Children Overcome Learning Difficulties, Jerome Rosner, 1993, Walker & Co. (ISBN 0-8027-7396-6)
> Although this book is not specific to a particular learning disability, it assists in the identification of particular problems which may occur with a broad range of academic difficulties. The author presents some excellent strategies for intervention and remediation.

How Brains Think, William H. Calvin, 1996, Basic Books
(ISBN 0-465-07278-X)
> Drawing on anthropology, evolutionary biology, linguistics, and the neurosciences, Calvin considers how a more intelligent brain developed using slow biological improvements over the last few million years. Although the author is a theoretical neurophysiologist, he writes in lay language which readers will appreciate.

Introducing Mind and Brain, Angus Gellatly and Oscar Zarate, 1999, Totem Books (ISBN 1-84046-005-9)
> The authors trace the historical development of ideas about the brain and its function from antiquity to the age of neuro-imaging. They explain what the sciences have to say about planning and action, language, memory, attention, emotions, and vision, and invite the reader to take a fresh look at the nature of mind, consciousness, and personal identity.

It's Nobody's Fault, Harold S. Koplewicz, 1996, Times Books (ISBN
0-8129-2473-8)

> The author addresses the biology of childhood disorders, as well as behavioral
> and emotional problems including anxiety, phobias, and so on. It contains good
> advice on the role of medication.

Learning Disabilities: A Family Affair, Betty B. Osman, 1979, Warner
Books (ISBN 0-446-35554-2)

> Although this book was written 20 years ago it is still an excellent resource. The
> author explains that a learning disability affects all aspects of the individual's life,
> and describes the impact on both the individual and the family. The author's
> compassion is apparent, and parents will find this a great support book. Although
> this book is currently out of print, the publisher plans on a reprint. An excellent
> book if you are able to locate a copy.

*Learning Disabilities and Psychosocial Functioning: A Neuropsychological
Perspective*, Byron P. Rourke and Darren R. Fuerst, 1991, Guilford Press
(ISBN 0-89862-767-2)

> The authors examine whether there is a cause and effect relationship between
> psychosocial dysfunction (anxiety, depression, and so on) and the pattern of
> neuropsychological assets and deficits of various learning disability subtypes,
> particularly NLD. The book presents both scientific research findings and
> numerous case studies which will be of interest to researchers, clinicians and
> educational specialists alike.

Learning To Learn, Carolyn Olivier and Rosemary F. Bowler, 1996,
Fireside, published by Simon & Schuster (ISBN 0-684-80990-7)

> The authors discuss in easy-to-understand language the nature of learning, how
> we process information and the various learning styles of students. They share
> many helpful ideas from organizational tips to test-taking strategies. The material
> is based on the program developed at Landmark College.

Left Brain – Right Brain: Perspectives from Cognitive Neuroscience, Sally P.
Springer and Georg Deutsch, 1997, W.H. Freeman & Co.
(ISBN 0-7167-3111-8)

> A very readable, science-based overview of brain asymmetry and its implications.
> It is also an excellent introduction to contemporary research on brain–behavior
> relationships. The authors discuss topics such as developmental disabilities, the
> nature of hemispheric specialization, disorders of speech and language, and the
> role of the right hemisphere in language.

The Misunderstood Child: Understanding and Coping With Your Child's Learning Disabilities, Larry Silver, 1998, Times Books (ISBN 0-81292-987-X)

    The author of this best-selling book has a wonderful understanding of the struggles faced by parents of a special needs child. He's also an expert at providing good, solid information in a manner that is both supportive and reader-friendly.

Negotiating the Special Education Maze: A Guide for Parents and Teachers, Winifred Anderson, Stephen Chitwood, and Deidre Hayden, 1990, Woodbine House (ISBN 0-933149-30-1)

    This is a must-read book for parents of learning disabled children in the US. It demystifies the world of special education, the legal rights of children, and the process parents may have to go through in order to secure appropriate services for their child. A great refresher book for even the veteran of the special education system.

A Neurodevelopmental Approach to Specific Learning Disorders, Kingsley Whitmore and Guy Willems (eds), 1999, Cambridge University Press (ISBN 1-898683-11-5)

    This book addresses neurodevelopmental disorders such as dyslexia, dyscalculia, dysgraphia, clumsiness, and other learning difficulties that are found within a school population. The editors present specific ideas about the causes of these disorders, along with practical information regarding clinical management.

Neuropsychological Assessment of Children: A Treatment-Oriented Approach, Byron P. Rourke, John L. Fisk, and John D. Strang, 1986, Guilford Press (ISBN 0-89862-676-5)

    The authors demonstrate how neuropsychological assessment can lead to successful intervention strategies. There are case studies and in-depth descriptions of a range of brain-related problems. This is an essential guide for the practitioner, as well as for anyone interested in this field of study.

Neuropsychology (Handbook of Perception and Cognition), Dahlia W. Zaidel (ed), 1994, Academic Press (ISBN 0-127752-90-0)

    Following a history of neuropsychology is a discussion of brain structure, function, and evolution; the neuropsychology of perceptual functions, attention, language, and emotion; the prefrontal cortex; movement sequencing disorders and apraxia; developmental aspects; aging and dementia; the creation and perception of art; sex differences in the brain; and neuropsychological rehabilitation. A technical but comprehensive.

The New Social Stories, Carol Gray, 1994, Future Horizons
(ISBN 1-885-47720-1)

> The author of the *Original Social Story Book*, provides 100 new 'social stories' based on the concept she introduced in her first book, and includes the Social Story Kit. It is not necessary to have read the original book in order to benefit from *The New Social Stories*.

No One to Play With: The Social Side of Learning Disabilities, Betty B. Osman, 1982, Academic Therapy Publications (ISBN 0-87879-687-8)

> This is a well-presented, no-nonsense book explaining that a learning disabled child's difficulties often affect their social skills. She refers to these difficulties as 'living disabilities' and explains that some children may not acquire social skills on their own. She suggests teaching them as you would an academic subject, concretely and specifically.

Nonverbal Learning Disabilities: The Syndrome and the Model, Byron P. Rourke, 1989, Guilford Press (ISBN 0-89862-378-2)

> This is clearly the most quoted book on the subject of NLD. Dr. Rourke explains the premise that NLD is caused by dysfunction of white matter in the brain, and shares his extensive research and findings. He defines the disorder, outlining the characteristics, dynamics and manifestations of NLD. Although technically written, and probably a difficult read for the layperson, it is worth the effort for anyone wanting a full understanding of this syndrome.

Original Social Story Book, Carol Gray, 1993, Future Horizons

> The author originally created the concept of 'social stories' for children who had difficulty processing daily situations which they encountered, particularly if they had a social component. Although often referred to as an autism intervention, this concept may be particularly helpful in assisting NLD youngsters gain or improve social skills, as well as deal more appropriately with novel situations.

Pervasive Developmental Disorders: Finding a Diagnosis and Getting Help, Mitzi Waltz, 1999, O'Reilly & Associates (ISBN 1-56592-530-0)

> The author presents an incredibly well-written manual, covering all of the issues associated with PDD-NOS. She first outlines the medical facts about the disorder, including a brief but very effective explanation of neurology, and moves on to getting a diagnosis.

Physiology of Behavior, Neil R. Carlson, 1998, Allyn & Bacon
(ISBN 0-205273-40-8)

> The revision of this classic book for professionals incorporates the latest discoveries in the rapidly changing fields of neuroscience and physiological psychology. Comprehensive research is combined with a coherent and

reader-friendly writing style. Topics covered include research, vision, body senses, chemical senses, movement, anxiety, autism, and more. Two new chapters on psychopharmacology and reinforcement and addiction have been added.

Pragmatic Language Intervention: Interactive Activities, Lynn S. Bliss, Thinking Publications (ISBN 0-930-59985-3)

This book covers specific communication skills as well as when each is to be used. The model dialogs will be very helpful for speech and language pathologists as well as teachers. As each communication skill is learned, it is then reinforced in everyday contexts. One of the most attractive features of this book is the numerous interactive activities and illustrations.

Pretending to be Normal, Liane Holliday Willey, 1999, Jessica Kingsley Publishers (ISBN 1-85302-749-9)

This is an autobiographical account by an adult with Asperger's syndrome. The author holds a doctorate degree in education, is a writer and researcher specializing in the fields of psycholinguistics and learning style differences, and is a wife and mother of three daughters, one of whom also has AS. Although written about AS, in many situations you will find the similarity to NLD remarkable. A beautifully written and poignant book that parents and family members will enjoy.

Raising A Thinking Child, Myrna B. Shure with Theresa Foy DiGeronimo, 1994, Henry Holt & Co. (ISBN 0-8050-2758-0)

The authors use the principles of interpersonal cognitive problem solving (ICPS) to teach appropriate skills and behavior. There are suggested dialogs, games, activities, and communication techniques which are designed for the parent to teach their child how to problem solve in a variety of situations.

Raising Careful, Confident Kids in a Crazy World, Paula Statman, 1999, Piccolo Press (ISBN 0-96400-422-4)

For parents of the naive, trusting NLD child, this book is particularly meaningful. Important safety issues are presented, as well as sample scripts to use with the child without instilling fear. The author uses a positive, straightforward approach to topics such as how to protect a child from molestation, abduction, and other dangerous situations.

Skillstreaming in Early Childhood: Teaching Prosocial Skills to the Preschool and Kindergarten Child, Ellen McGinnis and Arnold P. Goldstein, 1990, Research Press (ISBN 0-87822-321-5)

This book addresses the social skills deficits of youngsters, using techniques such as modeling, role-playing, and generalization of the skills. The authors have grouped the skills into six categories: Beginning Social Skills, School-Related

Skills, Friendship-Making Skills, Dealing with Feelings, Alternatives to Aggression, and Dealing with Stress.

Skillstreaming the Adolescent: New Strategies and Perspectives for Teaching Prosocial Skills (revised edn), Arnold P. Goldstein and Ellen McGinnis, 1997, Research Press (ISBN 0-87822-369-X)

This revised edition of an excellent book in the Skillstreaming series offers terrific information for implementing adolescent social skills lessons in the following categories: Beginning Social Skills, Advanced Social Skills, Dealing with Feelings, Alternatives to Aggression, Dealing with Stress, and Planning Skills.

Skillstreaming the Elementary School Child: New Strategies and Perspectives for Teaching Prosocial Skills, Ellen McGinnis and Arnold P. Goldstein, 1997, Research Press (ISBN 0-87822-373-8)

This selection in the Skillstreaming series focuses on teaching elementary-aged students how to deal with interpersonal conflicts and learn self-control through a curriculum of lessons in five areas: Classroom Survival Skills, Friendship-Making Skills, Dealing with Feelings, Alternatives to Aggression, and Dealing with Stress.

Socially Speaking: A Pragmatic Social Skills Program for Pupils with Mild to Moderate Learning Disabilities, Alison Schroeder, 1996, LDA (ISBN 1-855-03252-X)

The author presents a social skills program that is aimed at encouraging effective social interaction and improving self-esteem, listening skills, receptive and expressive language, and problem solving. The book includes a lesson plan for each week of the school year, each with a similar format. Assessment and evaluation procedures are included. The audience for this book is speech and language pathologists and teachers; however, parents will also find the content valuable.

The Source for Nonverbal Learning Disorders, (formerly titled *I Shouldn't Have to Tell You! A Guide to Understanding Nonverbal Learning Disorders*), Sue Thompson, 1997, LinguiSystems,

This is an absolute must-read book! It is the single best resource for parents and teachers of NLD kids – chock full of information and strategies. The author's depth of understanding of both the disorder and appropriate interventions will have you returning to it over and over again. Every parent of an NLD child should own this book.

Star Shaped Pegs, Square Holes: Nonverbal Learning Disorders and the Growing Up Years, Kathy Allen, 1996, Unicycle Press (e-mail the author at *Caitlin35@aol.com*)

This is a charming and warm book written to the middle school-aged NLD child to help them understand and cope with their disorder. There are great ideas and coping strategies throughout, written in a way that will appeal to the adolescent or young teen. The author suggests that it be read and understood with the support of a parent or professional.

Students With Learning Disabilities, Cecil D. Mercer, 1997, Prentice-Hall (ISBN 0-13-477176-1)

This textbook was written for application at the university level to teach an introductory class on learning disabilities. It provides extremely comprehensive coverage of the field of learning disabilities. Parents will benefit by reading it in order to gain an insight into how teachers are educated about various learning disabilities and are trained in classroom strategies.

Syndrome of Nonverbal Learning Disabilities: Neurodevelopmental Manifestations, Byron P. Rourke (ed), 1995, Guilford Press (ISBN 0-89862-155-0)

A collection of 18 contributions which explore the ramifications of NLD in the neuropsychology of learning disabilities and in pediatric neurological disease, disorder and dysfunction. Among the 15 diseases and disorders covered in the book are Callosal Agenesis's, Asperger's syndrome, Velocardiofacial syndrome, Sotos syndrome, Williams syndrome, and traumatic brain injury.

Taming the Recess Jungle, Carol Gray, 1993, Future Horizons (ISBN 1-885-47721-X)

The author tackles one of the major difficulties of young NLD children, the social challenges of school recess. Although the book is written for children with autism and related disorders, these children share the same social deficits as NLD youngsters. Ms. Gray identifies a variety of resources and materials which are helpful in simplifying the social demands of recess.

Teaching For The Two-Sided Mind: A Guide To Right Brain/Left Brain Education, Linda Williams, 1983, Simon & Schuster (ISBN 0-671-62239-0)

Although written for teachers, much of what is contained within this book is interesting for a wide audience. It approaches teaching from the perspective of the left brain, right brain, and whole brain. The author presents her material in simple language, and uses excellent examples to explain what can be a difficult topic to understand.

Teaching Your Child the Language of Social Success, Marshall P. Duke, Stephen Nowicki, Jr. and Elisabeth A. Martin, 1996, Peachtree Publishers, (ISBN 1-56145-126-6)

> The authors, who coined the term 'dysemia' to describe an inability to interpret and express nonverbal communications as the 'body language version of dyslexia,' have loaded this book with tips for improving nonverbal skills, from facial expressions, to space and touch, to gestures and postures. They also discuss how nonverbal language can be taught in a classroom setting.

Your Miracle Brain, Jean Carper, 2000, HarperCollins (ISBN 0-06-018391-8)

> This book was written as an informational rather than a medical guide to explain how the brain structure and functioning of brain cells can be improved by what you eat as well as the supplements you take.

When You Worry About the Child You Love: Emotional and Learning Problems in Children, Edward Hallowell, 1996, Simon & Schuster (ISBN 0-684-80090-X)

> There are a variety of disorders covered in this book, including specific information on NLD. This is an excellent, readable book with a host of wonderful and practical tips.

Wrightslaw: Special Education Law, Peter W.D. Wright and Pamela Darr Wright, 1999, Harbor House Law Press (ISBN 1-892320-03-7)

> This book is authored by the owners of the exceptional website for parents, attorneys, advocates, and educators known as Wrightslaw. This is the first in a planned series of special education law and advocacy books relating to the needs of children with disabilities. This book may be ordered through the authors' website at *www.wrightslaw.com*.

Appendix III

Internet Resources

All Kinds of Minds

All Kinds of Minds is a nonprofit organization formed to further the understanding of learning differences. The institute focuses on applied research, product development, program design, and professional training to increase the understanding and appropriate support for children with differences in learning. The work at this website is based upon the work of Dr. Mel Levine and his colleagues, and is a wonderful resource.

www.allkindsofminds.org

American Hyperlexia Association (AHA)

AHA is a nonprofit organization consisting of parents and family members of children with hyperlexia, speech and language and educational professionals, as well as other individuals interested in the mission to identify hyperlexia. This site has excellent information on hyperlexia and numerous articles on intervention.

www.hyperlexia.org

Anxiety Disorders Association of America (ADAA)

ADAA was formed to promote the prevention and cure of anxiety disorders. The association includes researchers and clinicians in the field of anxiety disorders, as well as anyone interested in developing a better understanding of these disorders. They have a very comprehensive website, which includes message boards and a chat facility.

www.adaa.org

Anxiety Disorders Education Program

The National Institute of Mental Health (NIMH) developed this program. The purpose is to educate the public and health care professionals about anxiety disorders, the fact that they are real medical illnesses, and that they can be effectively diagnosed and treated. The website has information on anxiety disorders, as well as treatment and many available resources.

www.nimh.nih.gov/anxiety

Asperger Syndrome Coalition of the United States (ASC-US)

ASC-US is a national nonprofit organization committed to providing the most up-to-date and comprehensive information on Asperger's syndrome and related conditions. Their website includes an NLD section.

www.asc-us.org

Canadian Hyperlexia Association

A group of concerned parents and professionals formed this organization. It is their mission to increase the awareness of hyperlexia and provide support for parents, children, and professionals. At their website you will find information as well as strategies for dealing with the disorder.

home.ican.net/~cha/

Child Neurology Home Page

This is a website which was formed to provide information on child neurology to professionals, patients and their families. It is an excellent resource in the field of pediatric neurology.

www.waisman.wisc.edu/child-neuro/index.html

Children and Adults with Attention Deficit/Hyperactivity Disorder (CHADD)

CHADD is a national nonprofit organization which was formed in 1987 by a group of parents. They represent both children and adults who have attention-deficit/hyperactivity disorder (AD/HD). Their mission is to provide education, advocacy, and support to individuals with AD/HD, and they have a very comprehensive website.

www.chadd.org

Council of Parent Attorneys and Advocates (COPAA)

An independent, nonprofit organization of attorneys, advocates, and parents established to improve the quality and quantity of legal assistance for parents of children with disabilities. At their website you will find useful legal information, as well as a directory of attorneys and advocates.

www.copaa.net

Developmental Delay Resources (DDR)

DDR is a nonprofit organization developed to support individuals working with children who have developmental delays. Their website provides information on various disorders, and intervention options.

www.devdelay.org

Dyspraxia Foundation

This organization was formed to support those affected by developmental dyspraxia. Developmental dyspraxia shares many characteristics with NLD. This website includes a description of the disorder and how it may affect the individual in school.

www.emmbrook.demon.co.uk/dysprax/homepage.htm

EDLAW

A website founded by S. James (Jim) Rosenfield, an attorney with almost 20 years of experience in special education law. This is a website devoted to special education law where you will find briefing papers and information on federal education laws.

www.edlaw.net

ERIC Clearinghouse on Adult, Career and Vocational Education (ERIC/ACVE)

ERIC stands for Educational Resources Information Center, and is sponsored by the US Department of Education, Office of Educational Research and Improvement (OERI), and administered by the National Library of Education (NLE). ACVE stands for adult, career, vocational and educational. ERIC/ACVE is located at the Center on Education and Training for Employment (CETE) at Ohio State University. This extensive website provides information on adult and continuing education, career education, and vocational and technical education including employment and training.

www.ericacve.org

ERIC Clearinghouse on Disabilities and Gifted Education (ERIC/EC)

ERIC stands for Educational Resources Information Center, and is sponsored by the US Department of Education, Office of Educational Research and Improvement (OERI), and administered by the National Library of Education (NLE). EC stands for Exceptional Children. This is one of sixteen federally funded clearinghouses. It is very large and extremely comprehensive, providing information on the education and development of individuals of all ages who have disabilities and/or who are gifted.

www.ericec.org

ERIC Clearinghouse on Elementary and Early Childhood Education (ERIC/EECE)

ERIC stands for Educational Resources Information Center, and is sponsored by the US Department of Education, Office of Educational Research and Improvement (OERI), and administered by the National Library of Education (NLE). It is a national information system designed to provide users with ready access to an extensive body of education-related literature. The EECE website is a very large, comprehensive site devoted to issues related to elementary and early childhood education.

www.ericeece.org

HEATH Resource Center

HEATH Resource Center of the American Council on Education is supported by the US Department of Education, and acts as a national clearinghouse providing information on post-secondary education for individuals with disabilities. This website is an excellent resource for issues affecting this population.

www.acenet.edu/programs/Access&Equity/HEATH

Job Accommodation Network (JAN)

The Job Accommodation Network is a toll-free consulting service providing information regarding job accommodations and the employment issues of people with disabilities, including information about the Americans with Disabilities Act (ADA). It is not a job placement service. This website has many links to disability related sites and information.

janweb.icdi.wvu.edu

LD OnLine

An exceptionally comprehensive learning disabilities website servicing parents, teachers and children. LD OnLine is a service of The Learning Project at WETA, Washington, DC, in association with The Coordinated Campaign for Learning Disabilities.

www.ldonline.org

Learning Disabilities Association of America (LDA)

The LDA is a national nonprofit organization supporting individuals with learning disabilities. Their website is very comprehensive and provides information on many types of learning disabilities and education law.

www.ldanatl.org

National Association of Private Schools for Exceptional Children (NAPSEC)

NAPSEC is a nonprofit organization made up of participating private special educational schools for children with disabilities. There are a links to all member school websites.

www.napsec.com

National Association of Protection and Advocacy System (NAPAS)

An association which represents federally mandated programs that protect the rights of people with disabilities.

www.protectionandadvocacy.com

National Attention Deficit Disorder Association (ADDA)

The ADDA is a nonprofit organization which is staffed entirely by unpaid volunteers to serve the needs of young adults and adults with ADD or ADHD. Their website is very comprehensive, with articles and interviews with some of the leading experts in the field.

www.add.org

National Center for Learning Disabilities (NCLD)

NCLD's mission is to promote public awareness and understanding of children and adults with learning disabilities, and to provide national leadership on their behalf so they may achieve their potential and enjoy full participation in our society. Their website has many full text articles, and an excellent links section to additional learning disability resources.

www.ncld.org

National Information Center for Children and Youth with Disabilities (NICHCY)

The national information and referral center that provides information on disabilities and disability-related issues for families, educators, and other professionals. Their special focus is children and youth, from birth to age 22. This website is quite large, with many articles, as well as resource sheets with state-specific information.

www.nichcy.org

NLD on the Web!

The most comprehensive NLD site on the web, and the official web presence of Byron P. Rourke, PhD, FRSC, and worldwide web headquarters of Sue Thompson, MA, CET. All of Ms. Thompson's work is on the site, as is Dr. Rourke's NLD Assessment Protocol and a Question and Answer section. The site is quite large, but designed so that it is easy to navigate, providing information for parents, professionals, and educators. There are numerous articles explaining NLD (grouped by reading difficulty), information on assessment, advocacy, and intervention, an extensive 'library' of other suggested reading, and a comprehensive calendar of seminars, workshops, and conferences on NLD and related topics. There is also a private forum allowing for the free exchange of information, and a chat facility.

www.nldontheweb.org

NLDLine

A website devoted to increasing awareness of NLD among parents and professionals. The site features articles and resource listings, personal stories, a bulletin board and a Pen Pals section for children with NLD.

www.nldline.com

OnLine Asperger Syndrome Information and Support (OASIS)

This incredibly comprehensive site for Asperger's syndrome (AS) is owned and operated by the parent of a child diagnosed with AS, a disorder which has remarkable similarities to NLD. This site has become synonymous with the name Asperger's syndrome, and has become a home, or 'oasis' for those interested in, or living with, AS.

www.aspergersyndrome.org

Recording for the Blind and Dyslexic (RFB&D)

A national nonprofit organization that serves people who cannot read standard print because of a visual, perceptual, or other physical disability. RFB&D is recognized as the nation's leading educational lending library of academic and professional textbooks on audiotape from elementary through postgraduate and professional levels. There is a search facility at their website so that you can key in information on a particular book and find out if it has been recorded and is available.

www.rfbd.org

School Psychology Resources Online

An extensive listing of school psychology resources for psychologists, parents, and educators, covering such subjects as learning disabilities, ADHD, functional behavioral assessment, autism, adolescence, parenting, psychological assessment, special education, and more.

www.schoolpsychology.net

Tera's NLD Jumpstation: A Resource on Nonverbal Learning Disabilities by an NLD Person

This site was created by Tera Kirk, a young woman with NLD, who is currently attending Agnes Scott College in Georgia. It provides an excellent and humorous description of NLD from the perspective of an individual with the disorder. A nice site to visit with your NLD adolescent or young teen to help them better understand their disorder.

www.geocities.com/HotSprings/Spa/7262

Wrightslaw: The Special Ed Advocate

For anyone needing accurate and up-to-date information on educational law or advocacy, this is the place. Parents, educators, experts, and attorneys visit this site for information about effective advocacy for children with disabilities. You'll find hundreds of articles, cases, newsletters, and other information about special education law and advocacy in the Wrightslaw Libraries.

www.wrightslaw.com

Appendix IV

Organizations

Alliance for Technology Access
2175 E Francisco Boulevard, Suite L
San Rafael, CA 94901
(800) 455-7970 or (415) 455-4575
E-mail: *atainfo@ataccess.org*
Web: *www.ataccess.org*

American Council on Rural Special Education (ACRES)
Kansas State University
2323 Anderson Avenue, Suite 226
Manhattan, KS 66502
(785) 532-2737
E-mail: *acres@ksu.edu*
Web: *www.ksu.edu/acres*

American Heart Association
7272 Greenville Avenue
Dallas, TX 75231
(800) 242-8721 or (214) 373-6300
E-mail: *inquire@amhrt.org*
Web: *www.americanheart.org*

American Hyperlexia Association (AHA)
195 W. Spangler, Suite B
Elmhurst, IL 60126
(630) 415-2212
E-mail: *president@hyperlexia.org*
Web: *www.hyperlexia.org*

American Occupational Therapy Association (AOTA)
4720 Montgomery Lane
PO Box 31220
Bethesda, MD 20824-1220
(301) 652-2682
E-mail: *helpdesk@aota.org*
Web: *www.aota.org*

American Physical Therapy Association (APTA)
1111 N Fairfax Street
Alexandria, VA 22314
(800) 999-2782 or (703) 684-2782
E-mail: *practice@apta.org*
Web: *www.apta.org*

American Speech-Language-Hearing Association (ASHA)
10801 Rockville Pike
Rockville, MD 20852
(800) 638-8255 or (301) 897-5700
E-mail: *actioncenter@asha.org*
Web: *www.asha.org*

American Therapeutic Recreation Association
PO Box 15215
Hattiesburg, MS 39404-5215
(800) 553-0304 or (601) 264-3413
E-mail: *atta@accessnet.com*
Web: *www.atra-tr.org*

Amicus for Children
1023 Old Swede Road
Douglassville, PA 19518
(610) 689-4226
E-mail: *amicusforchildren@att.net*
Web: *www.amicusforchildren.org*

Anxiety Disorders Association of America
11900 Parklawn Drive, #100
Rockville, MD 20852-2624
(301) 231-9350
E-mail: *AnxDis@aol.com*
Web: *www.adaa.org*

Council for Learning Disabilities
PO Box 40303
Overland Park, KS 66204
(913) 492-2546
E-mail: *webmaster@cldinternational.org*
Web: *http://www.cldinternational.org*

Easter Seals
230 W Monroe Street, Suite 1800
Chicago, IL 60606
(800) 221-6827 or (312) 726-6200
E-Mail: *nessinfo@seals.com*
Web: *www.easter-seals.org*

Epilepsy Foundation
4351 Garden City Drive, 5th Floor
Landover, MD 20785-4941
(800) 332-1000 or (301) 459-3700
E-mail: *postmaster@efa.org*
Web: *www.efa.org*

FACES: The National Craniofacial Association
PO Box 11082
Chattanooga, TN 37401
(800) 332-2372 or (423) 266-1632
E-mail: *faces@faces-cranio.org*
Web: *www.faces-cranio.org*

Family Resource Center on Disabilities
20 E Jackson Boulevard, Room 900
Chicago, IL 60604
(800) 952-4199 (IL only) or (312) 939-3513

Family Village
Waisman Center
University of Wisconsin-Madison
1500 Highland Avenue
Madison, WI 53705-2280
E-mail: *familyvillage@waisman.wisc.edu*
Web: *www.familyvillage.wisc.edu*

Federation of Families for Children's Mental Health
1021 Prince Street
Alexandria, VA 22314-2971
(703) 684-7710
E-mail: *ffcmh@ffcmh.com*
Web: *www.ffcmh.org*

Hydrocephalus Association
870 Market Street #955
San Francisco, CA 94102
(415) 732-7040
E-mail: *hydroassoc@aol.com*
Web: *www.hydroassoc.org*

Independent Living Research Utilization Project
The Institute for Rehabilitation and Research
2323 S Sheppard, Suite 1000
Houston, TX 77019
(713) 520-0232
E-mail: *ilru@ilru.org*
Web: *www.ilru.org*

International Dyslexia Association
(formerly The Orton Dyslexia Society)
Chester Building #382
8600 LaSalle Road
Baltimore, MD 21286-2044
(800) 222-3123 or (410) 296-0232
E-mail: *info@interdys.org*
Web: *www.interdys.org*

International Reading Association
800 Barksdale Road
PO Box 8139
Newark, DE 19714-8139
(302) 731-1600
E-mail: *www.pubinfo@reading.org*
Web: *www.reading.org*

International Rett Syndrome Association
9121 Piscataway Road, Suite 2B
Clinton, MD 20735-2561
(800) 818-7388 or (301) 856-3334
E-mail: *irsa@rettsyndrome.org*
Web: *www.rettsyndrome.org*

Learning Disabilities Association of America (LDA)

4156 Library Road
Pittsburgh, PA 15234
(888) 300-6710, (412) 341-1515, or (412) 341-8077
E-mail: *ldanatl@usaor.net*
Web: *www.ldanatl.org*

Leukemia Society of America

600 Third Avenue
New York, NY 10016
(800) 955-4572 or (212) 573-8484
E-mail: *infocenter@leukemia-lymphoma.org*
Web: *www.leukemia.org*

National Association for the Education of Young Children (NAEYC)

1509 16th Street NW
Washington, DC 20036
E-mail: *naeyc@naeyc.org*
Web: *www.naeyc.org*

National Association of Private Schools for Exceptional Children (NAPSEC)

1522 K Street NW, Suite 1032
Washington, DC 20005
(202) 408-3338
E-mail: *napsec@aol.com*
Web: *www.napsec.com*

National Association of Protection and Advocacy System (NAPAS)

900 Second Street NE, Suite 211
Washington, DC 20002
(202) 408-9514
E-mail: *napas@earthlink.net*
Web: *www.protectionandadvocacy.com*

National Attention Deficit Disorder Association

1788 Second Street, Suite 200
Highland Park, IL 60035
(847) 432-2332
E-mail: *mail@add.org*
Web: *www.add.org*

National Center for Learning Disabilities (NCLD)

381 Park Avenue S, Suite 1401
New York, NY 10016
(888) 575-7373 or (212) 545-7510
Web: *www.ncld.org*

National Clearinghouse for Alcohol and Drug Information (NCADI)

PO Box 2345
Rockville, MD 20847-2345
(800) 729-6686 or (301) 468-2600
E-mail: *info@health.org*
Web: *www.health.org*

National Fragile X Foundation

1441 York Street, Suite 303
Denver, CO 80206
(800) 688-8765 or (303) 333-6155
E-mail: *natlfx@sprintmail.com*
Web: *www.nfxf.org*

National Information Center for Children and Youth with Disabilities (NICHCY)

PO Box 1492
Washington, DC 20013-1492
(800) 695-0285 or (202) 884-8200
E-mail: *nichcy@aed.org*
Web: *www.nichcy.org*

National Institute on Deafness and Other Communication Disorders Clearinghouse

One Communication Avenue
Bethesda, MD 20892-3456
(800) 241-1044
E-mail: *nidcdinfo@nidcd.nih.gov*
Web: *www.nih.gov/nidcd/*

National Lead Information Center and Clearinghouse

8601 Georgia Avenue, Suite 503
Silver Spring, MD 20910
(800) 424-5323
E-mail: *hotline.lead@epa.gov*
Web: *www.epa.gov/lead*

National Mental Health Association
1021 Prince Street
Alexandria, VA 22314-2971
(800) 969-6642 or (703) 684-7722
E-mail: *nmhainfo@aol.com*
Web: *www.nmha.org*

National Neurofibromatosis Foundation
95 Pine Street 16th Floor
New York, NY 10005
(800) 323-7938 or (212) 344-6633
E-mail: *NNFF@aol.com*
Web: *www.nf.org*

National Organization on Fetal Alcohol Syndrome (NOFAS)
418 C Street NE
Washington, DC 20002
(800) 666-6327 or (202) 785-4585
E-mail: *nofas@erols.com*
Web: *www.nofas.org*

National Organization for Rare Disorders (NORD)
PO Box 8923
New Fairfield, CT 06812-8923
(800) 999-6673 or (203) 746-6518
E-mail: *orphan@nord-rdb.com*
Web: *www.nord-rdb.com/~orphan*

National Parent Network on Disabilities
1130 17th Street NW, Suite 400
Washington, DC 20036
(202) 463-2299
E-mail: *npnd@cs.com*
Web: *www.npnd.org*

National Parent to Parent Support and Information System
PO Box 907
Blue Ridge, GA 30513
(800) 651-1151 or (706) 374-3822
E-mail: *nppsis@ellijay.com*
Web: *www.nppsis.org*

National Scoliosis Foundation
5 Cabot Place
Stoughton, MA 02072
(800) 673-6922 or (781) 341-6333
E-mail: *NSF@scoliosis.org*
Web: *www.scoliosis.org*

Neurofibromatosis
8855 Annapolis Road, Suite 110
Lanham, MD 20706-2924
(800) 942-6825 or (301) 577-8984
E-mail: *NFInc1@aol.com*
Web: *www.nfinc.org*

Nonverbal Learning Disorders Association
PO Box 220
Canton, CT 06019-0220
(860) 693-3738
E-mail: *NLDResources@aol.com*
Web: *www.nlda.org*

OC Foundation (Obsessive Compulsive Disorder)
PO Box 70
Milford, CT 06460-0070
(203) 878-5669
E-mail: *info@ocfoundation.org*
Web: *www.ocfoundation.org*

Office of Special Education and Rehabilitative Services
Clearinghouse on Disability Information
Room 3132, Switzer Building
330 C Street SW
Washington, DC 20202-2524
(202) 205-8241
Web: *www.ed.gov/offices/OSERS*

President's Committee – Job Accommodation Network
West Virginia University
918 Chestnut Ridge Road, Suite 1
PO Box 6080
Morgantown, WV 26506-6080
(800) 526-7234 or (800) 232-9675
E-mail: *bloy@wvu.edu*
Web: *janweb.icdi.wvu.edu*

Recording for the Blind and Dyslexic (books on tape)
The Anne T. MacDonald Center
20 Roszel Road
Princeton, NJ 08540
(800) 221-4792 or (609) 452-0606
E-mail: *custserv@rfbd.org*
Web: *www.rfbd.org*

Rehabilitation Engineering and Assistive Technology Society of North America (RESNA)
1700 N. Moore Street, Suite 1540
Arlington, VA 22209-1903
(703) 524-6686
E-mail: *natloffice@resna.org*
Web: *www.resna.org*

Research and Training Center
Family Support and Children's Mental Health
Portland State University
PO Box 751
Portland, OR 97207-0751
(800) 628-1696 or (503) 725-4040
E-mail: *caplane@rri.pdx.edu*
Web: *www.rtc.pdx.edu*

Research and Training Center on Independent Living
University of Kansas
4089 Dole Building
Lawrence, KS 66045-2930
(785) 864-4095
E-mail: *rtcil@kuhub.cc.ukansas.edu*
Web: *www.lsi.ukans.edu/rtcil*

Sotos Syndrome Support Association
Three Danada Square East
PMB #235
Wheaton, IL 60187
(888) 246-7772
E-mail: *sssa@well.com*
Web: *www.well.com/user/sssa*

Special Olympics International
1325 G Street NW, Suite 500
Washington, DC 20005
(202) 628-3630
E-mail: *specialolympics@msn.com*
Web: *www.specialolympics.org*

Spina Bifida Association of America
4590 MacArthur Boulevard, NW, Suite 250
Washington, DC 20007-4226
(800) 621-3141 or (202) 944-3285
E-mail: *sbaa@sbaa.org*
Web: *www.sbaa.org*

Technical Assistance Alliance for Parent Centers (the Alliance)
PACER Center
4826 Chicago Avenue S
Minneapolis, MN 55417-1098
(888) 248-0822 or (612) 827-2966
E-mail: *alliance@taalliance.org*
Web: *www.taalliance.org*

Tourette Syndrome Association
42–40 Bell Boulevard
Bayside, NY 11361
(800) 237-0717 or (718) 224-2999
E-mail: *tourette@ix.netcom.com*
Web: *www.tourette-syndrome.com*

The Turner's Syndrome Society of the US
1313 SE 5th Street, Suite 327
Minneapolis, MN 55414
(800) 365-9944
E-mail: *webmaster@turner-syndrome-us.org*
Web: *www.turner-syndrome-us.org*

United Cerebral Palsy Association
1660 L Street NW, Suite 700
Washington, DC 20036
(800) 872-5827 or (202) 776-0406
E-mail: *ucpnatl@ucpa.org*
Web: *www.ucpa.org*

Williams Syndrome Association

1312 N Campbell, Suite 34
Royal Oak, MI
(248) 541-3630
E-mail: *TMonkaba@aol.com*
Web: *www.williams-syndrome.org/*

Bibliography

Arffa, S., Fitzhugh-Bell, K, and Black, W. (1989) 'Neuropsychological profiles of children with learning disabilities and children with documented brain damage.' *Journal of Learning Disabilities 22*, 635–640.

Asendorpf, J.B. (1993) 'Abnormal shyness in children.' *Journal of Child Psychology and Psychiatry 34*, 1069–1081.

Badian, N. (1983) 'Arithmetic and nonverbal learning.' *Progress in Learning Disabilities 5*, 235–264.

Badian, N. (1992) 'Nonverbal learning disability, school behavior, and dyslexia.' *Annals of Dyslexia 42*, 159–178.

Badian, N. and Ghublikian, M. (1982) 'The personal-social characteristics of children with poor mathematical computation skills.' *Journal of Learning Disabilities 16*, 154–157.

Baron, I.S. and Goldberger, E. (1993) 'Neuropsychological disturbances of hydrocephalic children with implications for special education and rehabilitation.' *Neuropsychological Rehabilitation, Special Issue: Issues in the Neuropsychological Rehabilitation of Children with Brain Dysfunction 3*, 4, 389–410.

Batchelor, E., Grey, J., and Dean, R.S. (1990) 'Neuropsychological aspects of arithmetic performance in learning disability.' *International Journal of Clinical Neuropsychology 12*, 90–94.

Battistia, M. (1980) 'Interrelationships between problem solving ability, right hemisphere processing facility and mathematics learning.' *Focus on Learning Problems in Mathematics 2*, 53–60.

Baum, K., Schulte, C., Girke, W., Reischies, F., and Felix, R. (1996) 'Incidental white-matter foci on MRI in "healthy" subjects: Evidence of subtle cognitive dysfunction.' *Neuroradiology 38*, 8, 755–760.

Bigler, E.D. (1989) 'On the neuropsychology of suicide.' *Journal of Learning Disabilities 22*, 3, 180–185.

Brookshire, B., Butler, I., Ewing-Cobbs, L., and Fletcher, J. (1994) 'Neuropsychological characteristics of children with Tourette syndrome: Evidence for a nonverbal learning disability?' *Journal of Clinical and Experimental Neuropsychology 16*, 2, 289–302.

Brumback, R.A., Harper, C.R., and Weinberg, W.A. (1996) 'Nonverbal Learning Disabilities, Asperger's syndrome, pervasive developmental disorder – should we care?' *Journal of Child Neurology 11*, 6, 427–429.

Brumback, R.A. and Staton, R.D. (1982a) 'An hypothesis regarding the commonality of right-hemisphere involvement in learning disability, attentional disorder, and childhood major depressive disorder.' *Perceptual Motor Skills 55*, 3, 1091–1097.

Brumback, R.A. and Staton, R.D. (1982b) 'Right hemisphere involvement in learning disability, attention deficit disorder, and childhood major depressive disorder.' *Medical Hypotheses 8*, 5, 505–514.

Casey, J.E., Rourke, B.P., and Picard, E. (1991) 'Syndrome of Nonverbal Learning Disabilities: Age differences in neuro-psychological, academic, and socioemotional functioning.' *Development and Psychopathology 3*, 329–345.

Chia, S.H. (1997) 'The child, his family and dyspraxia.' *Professional Care: Mother and Child 7*, 105–107.

Cohen, M.J., Branch, W.B., and Hynd, G.W. (1994) 'Receptive prosody in children with left or right hemisphere dysfunction.' *Brain and Language 47*, 2, 171–181.

Dean, R.S. (1983) 'Intelligence as a predictor of nonverbal learning with learning-disabled children.' *Journal of Clinical Psychology 39*, 3, 437–441.

Denckla, M.B. (1983) 'The neuropsychology of social-emotional learning disabilities.' *Archives of Neurology 40*, 461–462.

Denckla, M.B. (1991) 'Academic and extracurricular aspects of Nonverbal Learning Disabilities.' *Psychiatric Annals 21*, 12, 717–724.

Deuel, R.K. and Doar, B.P. (1992) 'Developmental manual dyspraxia: a lesson in mind and brain.' *Journal of Child Neurology 7*, 99–103.

Dimitrovsky, L., Spector, H., Levy-Shiff, R., and Vakil, E. (1998) 'Interpretation of facial expressions of affect in children with learning disabilities with verbal or nonverbal deficits.' *Journal of Learning Disabilities 32*, 3, 286–292.

Donders, J., Rourke, B.P., and Canady, A.I. (1991) 'Neuropsychological functioning of hydrocephalic children.' *Journal of Clinical and Experimental Neuropsychology 13*, 4, 607–613.

Ellis, H.D., Ellis, D.M., Fraser, W., and Deb, S. (1994) 'A preliminary study of right hemisphere cognitive deficits and impaired social judgements among young people with Asperger syndrome.' *European Child and Adolescent Psychiatry 3*, 255–266.

Fisher, N.J. and DeLuca, J.W. (1997) 'Verbal learning strategies of adolescents and adults with the syndrome of nonverbal learning disabilities.' *Child Neuropsychology 3*, 3, 192–198.

Fisher, N.J., DeLuca, J.W., and Rourke, B.P. (1997) 'Wisconsin Card Sorting Test and Halstead Category Test performances of children and adolescents who exhibit the syndrome of Nonverbal Learning Disabilities.' *Child Neuropsychology 3*, 61–70.

Fletcher, J.M. (1989) 'Nonverbal Learning Disabilities and suicide: Classification leads to prevention.' *Journal of Learning Disabilities 22*, 3, 176–179.

Foss, J.M. (1991) 'Nonverbal Learning Disabilities and remedial interventions.' *Annals of Dyslexia 41*, 128–140.

Fox, A.M. and Lent, B. (1996) 'Clumsy children: Primer on developmental coordination disorder.' *Canadian Family Physician 42*, 1965–1971.

Fuerst, D., Fisk, J.L and Rourke, B.P. (1990) 'Psychosocial functioning of learning-disabled children: Relations between WISC verbal IQ – performance IQ discrepancies and personality subtypes.' *Journal of Consulting and Clinical Psychology 58*, 657–660.

Gillberg, C. (1991) 'Pediatric neuropsychiatry.' *Current Opinion in Neurology and Neurosurgery 4*, 381–390.

Glosser, G. and Koppell, S. (1987) 'Emotional-behavioral patterns in children with learning disabilities: Lateralized hemispheric differences.' *Journal of Learning Disabilities 20*, 365–368.

Goldberg, E. and Costa, L.D. (1981) 'Hemisphere differences in the acquisition and use of asymmetries in the brain.' *Brain and Language 14*, 144–173.

Goldstein, D.B. (June 18, 2000) 'Children's Nonverbal Learning Disabilities Scale.' *Assessment page:* www.nldontheweb.org/Goldstein_1.htm

Gross-Tsur, V., Shalev, R.S., Manor, O., and Amir, N. (1995) 'Developmental right-hemisphere syndrome: Clinical spectrum of the nonverbal learning disability.' *Journal of Learning Disabilities 28*, 2, 80–86.

Harnadek, M. and Rourke, B.P. (1994) 'Principal identifying features of the syndrome of Nonverbal Learning Disabilities in children.' *Journal of Learning Disabilities 27*, 144–154.

Heller, W. (June 18, 2000) 'Understanding Nonverbal Learning Disability (NVLD).' *About NLD Page:* www.nldontheweb.org/heller.htm

Hulme, C. and Lord, R. (1986) 'Clumsy children: A review of recent research.' Child: Care, *Health and Development 12*, 4, 257–269.

Humphries, T. (1993) 'Nonverbal learning disabilities: A distinct group within our population.' *Communique*, LDA Ontario.

Johnson, D.J. (1987) 'Nonverbal Learning Disabilities.' *Pediatric Annals 16*, 2, 133–141.

Keith, R.W. (1996) 'Understanding central auditory processing disorders.' *The Hearing Journal 49*, 20–28.

Klin, A., Volkmar, F.R., Sparrow, S.S., Cicchetti, D.V., and Rourke, B.P. (1995) 'Validity and neuropsychological characterization of Asperger syndrome: Convergence with Nonverbal Learning Disabilities syndrome.' *Journal of Child Psychology and Psychiatry 36*, 7, 1127–1140.

Kopp, S. and Gillberg, C. (1992) 'Girls with social deficits and learning problems: Autism, atypical Asperger syndrome or a variant of these conditions.' *European Child and Adolescent Psychiatry 1*, 2, 89–99.

Kowalchuk, B. and King, J.D. (1989) 'Adult suicide versus coping with nonverbal learning disorder.' *Journal of Learning Disabilities 22*, 3, 177–178.

Levin, H., Scheller, J., Rickard, T., Grafman, J., Martinkowski, K., Winslow, M., and Mirvis, S. (1996) 'Dyscalculia and dyslexia after right hemisphere injury in infancy.' *Archives of Neurology 53*, 1, 88–96.

Little, L. (1998) 'Severe childhood sexual abuse and nonverbal learning disability.' *American Journal of Psychotherapy 52*, 3, 367–381.

Little, L. (1999) 'The misunderstood child: The child with a nonverbal learning disorder.' *Journal of the Society of Pediatric Nurses 4*, 3, 113–121.

Little, S.S. (1993) 'Nonverbal Learning Disabilities and socioemotional functioning: A review of recent literature.' *Journal of Learning Disabilities 26*, 10, 653–665.

Lord-Maes, J. and Janiece-Obrzut, J.E. (1996) 'Neuropsychological consequences of traumatic brain injury in children and adolescents.' *Journal of Learning Disabilities 29*, 609.

Loveland, K.A., Fletcher, J.M., and Bailey, V. (1990) 'Verbal and nonverbal communication of events in learning-disabled subgroups.' *Journal of Clinical and Experimental Neuropsychology 12*, 433–447.

Mattson, A.J., Sheer, D.E., and Fletcher, J.M. (1992) 'Electrophysiological evidence of lateralized disturbances in children with learning disabilities.' *Journal of Clinical and Experimental Neuropsychology 14*, 5, 707–716.

McKelvey, J.R., Lambert, R., Mottson, L., and Shevell, M.I. (1995) 'Right hemisphere dysfunction in Asperger's Syndrome.' *Journal of Child Neurology 10*, 310–314.

Minskoff, E. (1980a) 'Teaching approach for developing nonverbal communication skills in students with social perception deficits, Part 1: The basic approach and body language cues.' *Journal of Learning Disabilities 13*, 3, 118–124.

Minskoff, E. (1980b) 'Teaching approach for developing nonverbal communication skills in students with social perception deficits, Part 2: Proxemic, vocalic, and artifactual cues.' *Journal of Learning Disabilities 13*, 4, 203–208.

Miyahara, M. and Mobs, I. (1995) 'Developmental dyspraxia and developmental coordination disorder.' *Neuropsychology Review 5*, 245–268.

Musiek, F. (1986) 'Neuroanatomy, neurophysiology, and central auditory assessment: Part III: Corpus callosum and efferent pathways.' *Ear and Hearing 7*, 349–358.

Musiek, F., Golleghy, K., and Ross, M. (1985) 'Profiles of types of central auditory processing disorders in children with learning disabilities.' *Journal of Childhood Communication Disorders 9*, 43–63.

Nussbaum, N.L. and Bigler, E.D. (1986) 'Neuropsychological and behavioral profiles of empirically derived subgroups of learning-disabled children.' *International Journal of Clinical Neuropsychology 8*, 82–89.

Obrzut, J.E. and Hynd, G.W. (1987) 'Cognitive dysfunction and psychoeducational assessment in individuals with acquired brain injury.' *Journal of Learning Disabilities 20*, 596–602.

Ozols, E.J. and Rourke, B.P. (1988) 'Characteristics of young learning-disabled children classified according to patterns of academic achievement: Auditory-perceptual and visual-perceptual abilities.' *Journal of Clinical Child Psychology 17*, 44–52.

Poole, N. (1997) 'Remediation of nonverbal learning problems.' *The Educational Therapist 18*, 3.

Reeves, W.H. (1983) 'Right cerebral hemispheric function: Behavioral correlates.' *International Journal of Neuroscience 18*, 3–4, 227–230.

Reiff, H.B. and Gerber, P.J. (1990) 'Cognitive correlates of social perception in students with learning disabilities.' *Journal of Learning Disabilities 23*, 4, 260–262.

Roman, M.A. (1998) 'The syndrome of Nonverbal Learning Disabilities: Clinical description and applied aspects.' *Current Issues in Education 1*, 1, 1.

Rourke, B.P. (1988a) 'Socio-emotional disturbances of learning-disabled children.' *Journal of Consulting and Clinical Psychology 56*, 801–810.

Rourke, B.P. (1988b) 'Syndrome of Nonverbal Learning Disabilities: Developmental manifestations in neurological disease, disorder, and dysfunction.' *The Clinical 2*, 293–330.

Rourke, B.P. (1989) 'Nonverbal Learning Disabilities, socioemotional disturbance, and suicide: A reply to Fletcher, Kowalchuk, King, and Bigler.' *Journal of Learning Disabilities 22*, 3, 186–187.

Rourke, B.P. (1993) 'Arithmetic disabilities, specific and otherwise: A neuropsychological perspective.' *Journal of Learning Disabilities 26*, 4, 214–226.

Rourke, B.P. (2000) 'Neuropsychological and psychosocial subtyping: A review of investigations within the University of Windsor laboratory.' *Canadian Psychology 41*, 34–50.

Rourke, B.P. (June 18, 2000) 'Syndrome of nonverbal learning disabilitie: Assessment Protocols.' *Byron Rourke Page:* www.nldontheweb.org/nld_assmt_protocol.htm

Rourke, B.P. and Conway, J.A. (1997) 'Disabilities of arithmetic and mathematical reasoning: Perspectives from neurology and neuropsychology.' *Journal of Learning Disabilities 30*, 1, 34–46.

Rourke, B.P., Dietrich, D.M., and Young, G.C. (1973) 'Significance of WISC verbal-performance discrepancies for younger children with learning disabilities.' *Perceptual and Motor Skills 36*, 275–282.

Rourke, B.P. and Finlaysen, M.A.J. (1978) 'Neuropsychological significance of variations in patterns of academic performance: Verbal and visual-spatial abilities.' *Journal of Abnormal Child Psychology 6*, 121–133.

Rourke, B.P. and Fisk, J.L. (1981) 'Socio-emotional disturbances of learning disabled children: The role of central processing deficits.' *Bulletin of the Orton Society 31*, 77–88.

Rourke, B.P. and Fuerst, D. (1996) 'Psychosocial dimensions of learning disability subtypes.' *Assessment 3*, 3, 277–290.

Rourke, B.P. and Strang, J.D. (1978) 'Neuropsychological significance of variations in patterns of academic performance: Motor, psychomotor, and tactile-perceptual abilities.' *Journal of Pediatric Psychology 2*, 62–66.

Rourke, B.P. and Tsatsanis, K.D. (1996) 'Syndrome of Nonverbal Learning Disabilities: Psycholinguistic assets and deficits.' *Topics in Language Disorders 16*, 2, 30–44.

Rourke, B.P., Young, G.C., and Flewelling, R.W. (1971) 'The relationships between WISC verbal-performance discrepancies and selected verbal, auditory-perceptual, visual-perceptual, and problem-solving abilities in children with learning disabilities.' *Journal of Clinical Psychology 27*, 475–479.

Rourke, B.P., Young, G.C., and Leenaars, A.A. (1989) 'A childhood learning disability that predisposes those afflicted to adolescent and adult depression and suicide risk.' *Journal of Learning Disabilities 22*, 3, 169–175.

Schatz, J., Craft, S., Koby, M., and Park, T.S. (1997) 'Associative learning in children with perinatal brain injury.' *Journal of the International Neuropsychological Society 3*, 6, 521–527.

Semrud-Clikeman, M. and Hynd, G.W. (1990) 'Right hemispheric dysfunction in Nonverbal Learning Disabilities: Social, academic, and adaptive functioning in adults and children.' *Psychological Bulletin 107*, 196–209.

Shields, J. (1991) 'Semantic-pragmatic disorder: A right hemisphere syndrome?' *British Journal of Disorders of Communication 26*, 383–392.

Sisterhen, D.H. and Gerber, P.J. (1989) 'Auditory, visual, and multisensory nonverbal social perception in adolescents with and without learning disabilities.' *Journal of Learning Disabilities 22*, 4, 245–249.

Spreen, O. (1989) 'The relationship between learning disabilities, emotional disorders, and neuropsychology: Some results and observations.' *Journal of Clinical and Experimental Neuropsychology 11*, 117–140.

Stellern, J., Marlowe, M., Jacobs, J., and Cosairt, A. (1985) 'Neuropsychological significance of right hemisphere cognitive mode in behavior disorders.' *Behavioral Disorders 2*, 113–124.

Stone, W.L. and LaGreca, A.N. (1984) 'Comprehension of nonverbal communication: A re-examination of the social competencies of learning-disabled children.' *Journal of Abnormal Child Psychology 12*, 505–518.

Strang, J.D. and Rourke, B.P. (1983) 'Concept-formation/non-verbal reasoning abilities of children who exhibit specific academic problems with arithmetic.' *Journal of Clinical Child Psychology 12*, 33–39.

Suzuki, L.A. and Leton, D.A. (1989) 'Spontaneous talkers among students with learning disabilities: Implications of right cerebral dysfunction.' *Journal of Learning Disabilities 22*, 6, 397–399.

Thompson, N.M., Francis, J.D., Steubing, K.K., and Fletcher, J.M. (1994) 'Motor, visual spatial, and somatosensory skills after closed head injury in children and adolescents: A study of change. *Neuropsychology 8*, 333–342.

Thompson, S. (1996) 'Nonverbal learning disorders.' Fall, *The Gram*, LDA-CA. Publication of the East Bay Learning Disabilities Association.

Thompson, S. (1997) 'Nonverbal learning disorders.' *The Gram*, Winter.

Thompson, S. (1998) 'Stress, anxiety, panic, and phobias: Secondary to NLD.' *The Gram*, Spring.

Tranel, D., Hall, L.E., Olson, S., and Tranel, N.N. (1987) 'Evidence for a right-hemisphere developmental learning disability.' *Developmental Neuropsychology 3*, 113–127.

Tsatsanis, K.D., Fuerst, D.R., and Rourke, B.P. (1997) 'Psychosocial dimensions of learning disabilities: External validation and relationship with age and academic functioning.' *Journal of Learning Disabilities 30*, 490–502.

Voeller, K.K. (1986) 'Right hemisphere deficit syndrome in children'. *American Journal of Psychiatry 143*, 1004–1009.

Voeller, K.K., Hanson, J.A., and Wendt, R.N. (1988) 'Facial affect recognition in children: A comparison of the performance of children with right and left hemisphere lesions.' *Neurology 38*, 11, 1744–1748.

Weintraub, S. and Mesulam, M.M. (1983) 'Developmental learning disabilities of the right hemisphere: Emotional, interpersonal, and cognitive components.' *Archives of Neurology 40*, 463–468.

Wiig, E.H. and Harris, S.P. (1974) 'Perception and interpretation of nonverbally expressed emotions by adolescents with learning disabilities.' *Perceptual and Motor Skills 38*, 239–245.

Williams, D.L., Gridley, B.E., and Fitzhugh-Bell, K. (1992) 'Cluster analysis of children and adolescents with brain damage and learning disabilities using neuropsychological, psychoeducational, and sociobehavioral variables.' *Journal of Learning Disabilities 25*, 5, 290–299.

Willoughby, C. and Polatajko, H.J. (1995) 'Motor problems in children with developmental coordination disorder: Review of the literature.' *American Journal of Occupational Therapists 49*, 787–794.

Wills, K.E. (1993) 'Neuropsychological functioning in children with spina bifida and/or hydrocephalus.' *Journal of Clinical Child Psychology, Special Issue: The Neuropsychological Basis of Disorders Affecting Children and Adolescents 22*, 2, 247–265.

Worling, D.E., Humphries, T., and Tannock, R. (1999) 'Spatial and emotional aspects of language inferencing in Nonverbal Learning Disabilities.' *Brain and Language 70*, 2, 220–239.

Index